If you are familiar with contemporary Non-duality teachings and looking for the next step (and there is one), take it with Jonathan Harrison who shows himself here to be a sure guide.
William Wildblood, author of *Meeting the Masters* (Axis Mundi Books)

There are no idle words in this book. Everything here has been tested in the fire. May this book bring you to THIS and to Authentic Doing.
Julian Daizan Skinner, Zen Master and founder of Zenways.org

Being 'aware', without effort, is the purest manifestation of our energy or 'Mana' as the Polynesians call it – which is to harness the true power of all there is. *YOU are THIS* lays bare the what, the how the when and the why of this process, inviting you to experience life from a truly cosmic perspective.
Barbara Meiklejohn-Free, Shaman and best-selling author of *The Shaman Within* and *The Book of Destiny* (Moon Books)

As a Reiki Master, I seek to channel the very essence so aptly revealed in this book.
Gaetano Vivo, Reiki Master and author of *Messages from the Angels of Transparency* (Axis Mundi Books)

A thought provoking read for those serious about the next age of human evolution.
Stephanie J. King, Soulpreneur™ and author of *Divine Guidance* (6th Books)

J.M. Harrison's new book *YOU are THIS* is a complete delight. Clearly distilled and insightful, it takes you on an expansive journey into the heart of true spiritual awareness. THIS is such a treasure of a book you will want to keep it close to you, possibly by your bedside, for a long time to come.

Nikki de Carteret, author of *Soul Power* (O-Books)

YOU are THIS

Awakening to the
Living Presence of Your Soul

YOU are THIS

Awakening to the
Living Presence of Your Soul

J.M. Harrison

MANTRA
BOOKS

Winchester, UK
Washington, USA

First published by Mantra Books, 2016
Mantra Books is an imprint of John Hunt Publishing Ltd., Laurel House, Station Approach,
Alresford, Hants, SO24 9JH, UK
office1@jhpbooks.net
www.johnhuntpublishing.com
www.mantra-books.net

For distributor details and how to order please visit the 'Ordering' section on our website.

Text copyright: J.M. Harrison 2015

ISBN: 978 1 78535 098 6
Library of Congress Control Number: 2015943100

A CIP catalogue record for this book is available from the British Library.

Design: Lee Nash

Printed in the USA by Edwards Brothers Malloy

We operate a distinctive and ethical publishing philosophy in all
areas of our business, from our global network of authors to
production and worldwide distribution.

CONTENTS

THIS... a poem

If I could give you anything
It would be THIS...
This instance, this feeling, this reality
For THIS is all we are.
I would give you myself
And in giving myself
You would recognise your own Self
Which is one and the same.
If I would show you true love
I would not give you a kiss
But I would bare you my Soul...
Share it with you.
And if I could do one more thing
Before I leave this place
I would give you my all
I would give you...
THIS...

© 2007 J.M. Harrison

Some there are that prize Non-dualism, others hold to dualism.
They know not the Truth, which is above both.

Advadhuta Gita (1.34)

∞ Acknowledgements ∞

LOVE and THANKS as always to my family for allowing me the time and space to write this book. W, H and G. XXX

Special thanks to *Christopher Pogioli* for his patient reading and wholehearted assistance in the copy editing process.

I am very grateful to *Julian Daizan Skinner* for finding time in his busy schedule to write the foreword for YOU are THIS.

Thanks to *John Hunt Publishing* for their continued support, and to everyone at Mantra Books who contributed their time and energy in the making of this book.

∞ Foreword ∞

by Julian Daizan Skinner (Juran Daizan 寿鸞 大山)

The monk Nangaku Ejo (677-744CE) travelled through the mountains to study with Eno, the sixth Zen ancestor. Eno greeted his arrival with, "What is this?" The young monk was speechless. He spent the next eight years with the question before coming to an awakening and becoming the sixth ancestor's successor.

I well remember my own teacher, Shinzan Miyamae Roshi, meeting me eye-to-eye in the interview room with, "Kore nanzo?" (What is this?) Because I have seen something of the value of this question, I'm delighted that my dear friend Jonathan Harrison invited me to write the foreword for his new book, "YOU are THIS".

I've largely experienced Jonathan in the context of him emerging from a remote rural paradise to run a busy retreat centre, providing a safe environment in which others could fall apart gracefully, an arena in which any but the most practical approach will inevitably fail. He'd spent many years in inner work quite as earnestly as Ejo, the monk above, and was called to practical application. I remain deeply impressed by Jonathan's grounding in his own spiritual truth and willingness to move heaven and earth so that others could find theirs. In long discussions together we explored the importance of spiritual service, of grounding. I remember sharing with him the image from Zen that after climbing the "mountain of awareness", you keep right on walking down the other side, "returning to the world". Jonathan, faced day-to-day with examples of ungrounded spirituality, wholeheartedly agreed.

Having seen Jonathan's spirituality expressed day-to-day through practicality, flexibility and humour, it's deeply gratifying that he has taken some time to share with us the corresponding inner lessons and understandings. There are no idle words in this book. Everything here has been tested in the fire.

We all know that we live in dangerous times. As a species we have become so successful that our very numbers undermine the integrity of the environment that sustains us. Our instincts for survival and reproduction paradoxically make us less likely to do either. As long as we live in the world of separation, the "Mego" as Jonathan so aptly puts it, our issues seem intractable. It is possible, and in fact not that difficult, to shift the awareness to realise the fundamental perfection of where we are right now – to recognise that actually we never left the Garden of Eden. This may be an important step on our journey, but in itself it contains no motive for action. We must move on to discover what Jonathan calls, "The sacredness of duality", and further still. My teacher's previous website was called, "Not-one; not-two.com" We can enter a place of "no fixed abode". In this place Jonathan challenges us to find, "Authentic Doing from Universal Being, and that is the most transformative and powerful Action that can take place in our world."

May this book bring you to THIS and to Authentic Doing. May you live in joy and be a source of joy. May your life benefit all.

About Daizan

Julian Daizan Skinner is the first Englishman to go to Japan and become a Roshi or Zen Master in the rigorous Rinzai tradition of Zen. Over twenty years ago, he gave up a promising career as a scientist in the pharmaceuticals industry, sold his house, gave all the money away and entered a Zen monastery. Over many years of strict training, in Japan and the west, Daizan Roshi received Dharma Transmission and permission to teach in both the Rinzai and Soto lineages of Zen. He has also undergone training as an enlightenment intensive master with Lawrence Noyes, leading student of the creator of enlightenment intensives, Charles Berner. Daizan Roshi received inka from Shinzan Miyamae Roshi of Gyokuryuji, with whom he continues to study. For more information on teacher training, retreats and more please visit: www.Zenways.org

∞ Preface ∞

I am simply here sharing Awareness, for I realise THIS to be the coreless core of *what* I am, *what-YOU-really-are* and what all essentially *IS*.

From THIS, there is a natural propensity to love and share, for THIS is realised to permeate, animate and integrate all life.

During the years 1997-2007, and without "better living through chemistry" as Ram Dass calls it, I underwent a series of expansive states of consciousness which eventually led to duality fading and Non-dual Awareness 'appearing' as if by magic. For a time, individual consciousness dissolved in the vibrant mysterious silence of Universal Awareness, the ocean of unmodified Consciousness. I glimpsed into, and merged with, *our* anonymous core, a truly liberating freedom. The resulting 'experience' was one of seeing and being an empty yet full aliveness which encompassed everything… and nothing. And in time, from out of the dynamic unified stillness, a thought arose – the primary thought "I AM".

From that dissolution in Awareness, I eventually 'came back' into the world and followed a healthy, natural inclination to learn, follow and live what had been seen and 'experienced'. Initially it felt as if a silent warm blanket of Intelligent Love, comfort and peace was wrapped around me, holding me, reassuring me, and nurturing me.

I described what took place as best I could in my second book, *Naked Being – Undressing your Mind, Transforming your Life;*

The human struggle is a search for Wholeness. We spend our lives trying to be complete. We begin by accumulating as much material wealth, status, power, honour and conditioned versions of 'success' as we possibly can, but in the end all of these are found to be lacking. None of them can be sustained, for they are mind made creations.

We realise that the meaning we seek is never going to be found outside of ourselves, and so we begin to search inside. When we delve deeply into our core, we find that our inner being is mystifyingly empty - empty of self. Within this emptiness, the fullness of LIFE is uncovered. From this Non-dual awakening we see all 'things' as illusory because the world of form is recognised to be fleeting and in a sense 'unreal'. As awareness deepens, a real grounding and balancing of the poles of being occurs. The Non-dual Spirit becomes established in the duality of the body and the world, providing a practical way for Naked Being to manifest. A rounded Wholeness arises from accepting the outer self to be the way your Non-dual Nature is released into the world. You now know yourself to be a unique individual following the ONE essence of LIFE called Spirit.

That's why YOU are THIS is presented in two parts. In part one, we take the journey from the individual to the Universal, or from duality to Non-duality. To help facilitate that step, I constantly use the little word THIS as a transformative tool, a catalyst for glimpsing Non-dual Awareness, *our* shared fundamental Reality. So the first part of the book continually returns the wandering mind to THIS – the unchanging and unchangeable Universal Awareness.

And yet that recognition of our essential unity is not 'it' – not the end of the story, but rather the opening to an intuitive, all-inclusive consciousness which naturally benefits the whole. For I began to see that Non-duality without the presence of an Authentic Individual was about as helpful as an offer of refreshment, when the cup you are handed is completely empty. This is because, although the meeting of the individual ego with Universal Awareness may bring about the end of the idea of seeking, a 'new' chapter in consciousness also emerges if we remain open and available. The Non-dual 'experience' is not the end, but rather a 'new' beginning. We begin to realise we are here to fall in love with life – so that we can really live it to the full, and wholeheartedly contribute to the Whole in our own unique way.

The grounding and integration of Non-duality is what awakens human consciousness to the existence of the Universal-Individual, or *Unividual* – a wholistically-minded being integrated in Wholeness. That is not to say perfected and complete, but Whole in the sense of aware of and in touch with all parts of one's being. In Wholeness, there is no negation or denial of any part of whom or what we are. We are Animal and Divine, warts and all. That is our hybrid reality – and that is what we constantly overlook.

So in part two, we journey to the Unividual. The Unividual is an aware, Authentic, peace-loving human being, attuned to the dimensions of form and formlessness and naturally empowered to share and express the transparency of what and who they are. For the Unividual, nothing is finished, perfected or complete, and yet higher and lower versions of identity and non-identity converge, establishing an expansive co-creative consciousness which is comfortably 'mine' and 'not mine'. There is now the presence of a very real 'me' arising out of the Non-dual 'me-less-ness'. Both are paradoxically present as One. This is the sacred convergence, the reflection back into the dual world of *our* Non-dual Awareness, and the presently emerging paradigm of human consciousness called *One-duality*.

The Unividual enduringly senses the coreless core of Non-dual Awareness – and with it comes the realisation that the many are the One, characterized in the world through multiplicity. It is called One-dual because the One is seen in the many, and the many is seen to be the One. It is not based in denial or negation but lived through an all-inclusive and grounded acceptance of the Whole. One-duality is the Non-dual One consciously expressed through duality. Now duality is realised to be as sacred as Non-duality. The seeking of any 'other' has ended, as has dependency on the idea of not seeking, for the once invisible treasure of the Unividual has been uncovered. Seeking and not seeking are no longer present, for the Unividual is living the presence of their Authentic Soul. Acceptance and surrendering to THIS is the next stepping stone in the evolution of human consciousness.

We are all moving, expanding, growing into the presently emerging paradigm of One-duality, an evolutionary step which is all-inclusive, creative and continuous. There is Intelligent Love shining bright within you in this very moment, an all-accepting loving consciousness directly reflecting the Wholeness, harmony and joy emanating from *our* core. Now is the time to allow and express THIS.

If you have an overwhelming feeling you want to change the world, then go on… do so. Change yourself. Uncover 'what' YOU are, and be the 'who' only You can be. The same origin as any other, always equal in value, yet unique and You. THIS is Wholeness. Personal transformation (Change) will naturally bring about Authentic Action through Love. There is no other way. All other forms of change are disconnected and temporary, as we have witnessed countless times in world history.

THIS is the key to your unique and sacred role, *our* Universal Truth, and the vital stepping stone to a flourishing world consciousness based in integrity, healing and Wholeness.

You are here on Earth at a crucial time in human history, and your vital role is to uncover how Awareness manifests in the world as You – for in truth there is no greater contribution and no more meaningful gift than THIS.

JMH – 2015

∞ Glossary of Terms ∞

Throughout the text certain words are capitalised to denote their significance and authenticity. The descriptions below are pointers to help guide you and are by no means intended to suggest complete or absolute definitions.

Authentic: from the origin, as expressed through human consciousness. An Authentic Human Being acts from an all-inclusive sense of Wholeness.

Heart Stream of Consciousness: the natural 'flow' of Universal Intelligence. Once an individual aligns with this ever-present 'stream', then inner and outer being have merged and Authentic Doing occurs in the form of Change and Action. Love, compassion and transformation are all manifestations of this eternal 'flow', as is the power to Act from and for the Whole.

Intelligent Love: one of the two primary qualities of Awareness. Universal existence itself is an expression of Intelligent Love in the form of life, order and beauty.

Knowingness: the spontaneous intuitive recognition of what IS, appearing in consciousness when personal belief and knowledge are transcended. Unavoidable Truth as it is, without participation or deliberation.

Peace of Mind: the second primary quality of Awareness. Along with Intelligent Love, this is equivalent to the *Being-Consciousness-Bliss*. This sublime experience is a glimpse of our shared fundamental infinite Reality.

Mego: individual human consciousness which denies our

essential Oneness. The 'I' or 'me' which persistently distinguishes itself from others. Mistakenly thinks duality to be the whole. An incomplete state of being lived and expressed through the partiality of an individuated mind. A divided sense of reality and a 'split' consciousness. It is sustained and fed by its own sense of separation. The individual mind, self, soul, and the part without awareness of the Whole.

Non-duality: the indivisible Universal non-persona of non-separation, with no subject and no object. The 'experienced awareness' of *what-YOU-really-are*, the Sole Cosmic Constant of the SELF. The Whole without the parts. The what without the who.

One-duality: the next stage in the evolution of human consciousness. From a Non-dual grounding there arises Unividual being. In this consciousness, the dual and the Non-dual are lived and experienced without attachment and the true Wholeness of One-duality is apparent. The all-inclusive human experience. The who and the what. Your Self, Soul, the part and the Whole. The Whole-part.

Patterning: the personal programme of thoughts, memories and emotions instinctively used by the individual mind of mego. Habitual mind content brought about by life circumstances, experiences or karmic conditioning.

Peace of Mind: another primary quality of Awareness or Being. In the true Non-dual experience, the mind is empty and silent, yet full and vibrant.

self, SELF and Self: these descriptions are used to clarify mego (dual), Awareness (Non-dual) and Soul (One-dual). The self sees the SELF as unreal. The SELF reveals duality as illusory. Your Authentic Self, the Unividual Soul sees and lives both, inhabiting space, matter and time while eternally bound to Oneness.

soul, Soul: the soul of the mego (little 's') is hidden, dormant or at most seldom present as the foreground of one's consciousness. From the Non-dual experience of Awareness, consciousness is awakening to the presence of the Authentic Soul (capital 'S').

Soulness: the nature, quality and consciousness of the Soul as lived by the Unividual persona.

THIS: what and who you are, what we all are, and all IS. The all-inclusive Reality. Not one, not two, but both and beyond. No limits. No non-limits. Simply THIS.

Unividual: the Universal-Individual. The persona who lives the Non-dual in the duality of the world, while ever-conscious all is the One.

Wholeness: the integration of human consciousness into one overseeing awareness. Acceptance of all possibilities and open to the infinite cycles of experience and growth. Conscious of all dimensions of the Body-Mind-Spirit being.

Worldview consciousness: the current globally accepted view of ourselves, life and others which is constantly changing and evolving.

you: the mego's partial identification with consciousness. Alone, divided and incomplete it is the self and the soul.

You: the consciousness of the Authentic Self. Individuality inseparable from Universality. The One-dual consciousness presently emerging in the world. In this text it is referred to as the Self or Soul.

YOU: the coreless core and presence of *what-YOU-really-are.* The Universal. Awareness, Consciousness, Brahman, the Absolute or Spirit. It is the One True SELF.

Part One

What

1

∞ THIS Kingdom is Within You ∞

What you are looking for is found within. But the paradox is, once you find it within, you realise that it's here, there, and everywhere. It's in the space directly in front of you now, in the stars floating across the night sky, and in the depths of planet Earth, for THIS is the foundation, substance and all-permeating Life-force of everything and nothing.

It's always closer than you think, because THIS is beyond thought. It's THIS – the here and now before you engage in thought. And yet, you can know and live THIS. For when the individual strips away the superfluous mental and emotional dross and merges with the Awareness of Universal presence, subject and object fade, and all is realised to be the One inseparable and indivisible THIS. And although it often seems hidden, it is no secret. It will cost you nothing, and everything. But if you really look with all your heart, you will find THIS, the Truth of *what* YOU are, the One True SELF.

We human beings have been seeking a deeper sense of identity for thousands of years. When guided by the ego, we have outwardly searched high and low, overlooking the Truth at *our* core. For within each one of us, there is the Divine ever-present foundation of Life itself, which can be glimpsed should we have the courage and determination to let go and dive into the depths of inner-being.

Throughout history, increasing numbers have suggested that what we are all seeking is THIS, the here and now – the transcendental Reality of Consciousness. It is here and now in you – but do you know that to be true? For it is one thing to understand, say or think, another to believe or hope, but to really know THIS means simply to realise it. Then it will no longer be an opinion you cling to, but an unshakeable Truth which simply IS. And although THIS is always here, that doesn't mean there is no need for you to look for it. For if you look deeply, with all your heart and soul, one day you will find THIS and the looking will be over, because there will be no seeker. The question of seeking something 'other' will no longer arise. You will realise and live THIS.

Awakening to the Awareness of the One True SELF arises from the individual diving into the Universal. The consequences of THIS are always the same, yet explained in a myriad of ways according to a number of factors; the timeline in history, the culture, philosophy, the individual's education and more. None of these matter in the end, for the fundamental and consistent message repeatedly reminds us there is only One Awareness, Source, Essence, Consciousness, Brahman, SELF, God from which all apparent forms arise. We share a unified ever-present 'coreless core' which is both the basis and content of all that IS.

Remembering THIS (the Awareness of *what-YOU-really-are*) requires courage and commitment, for it is deeply challenging to face and accept the embedded mental and emotional patterns and personal glitches accrued in the comings and goings of life. But if you begin to accept what appears in your mind rather than choosing to avoid it, then you will be heading in the 'right' direction for you will be facing what *you* need to face and letting go of what is truly in *your* way. Of course letting go is not as simple as dropping a banana skin into a bin, but with courage, effort, time and space, these self-addictive patterns lose their hypnotic power to dominate your consciousness, and eventually fade away like imaginary ghosts into the nothingness from which they came. Then Universal Awareness is realised to be the ever-present anonymous THIS because all forms and layers of separation are seen through. Unlike the sporadic patterns of the mind THIS does not come and go, because it is constant, insepa-rable and always here. So from the introspective action of emptying the wandering mind of ego, you uncover THIS.

THIS is always present, always here and now. The very belief that there is a separate somewhere 'else' or 'an-other time' to find THIS, is itself the misleading thought. There is nowhere 'else' to go 'to', and nothing 'other' to 'get', which is all very disappointing for an individual mind firmly rooted in seeking and separation. As this isolated state of individuality and disconnected mind derives its identity from the perspective of the 'me', for clarity's sake, let's call it the *mego*.

Of course, there is work to do for the mego, but no 'other' can tell you the detail of that work, for the crux of it is whatever arises in *your* mind. Those addictive self-revolving patterns and obstacles are there for very good reason. The wonderful 'loving' reality is that the undoing of those same obstructions allows us to glimpse THIS... and more.

The non-conceptual Awareness of THIS is inconceivable to the conceptually-based mego. Perhaps more distressing for the mego still, is that at the coreless core of *what-YOU-really-are*, there is no sense of 'I', for the One True SELF of Awareness is anonymous and 'I-less'. At the Heart of Consciousness, there is not even a sense of 'we' or 'us' – for underneath all imagined identity, invention and pretence, Awareness is simply the eternal infinite THIS. It is non-desiring choice-less Being and timeless Truth.

Some believe that killing the mego is the way. And yet it is clear that real and lasting Change only comes from Love, so the answer must be to love it to bits. Some hold fast to the belief that individuality, character and uniqueness have little or no role in spiritual fulfilment, believing that should we see THIS, then we would reach the finality of being 'awakened' and therefore be, look and act in certain stereotypical ways. But is that an Authentic experience or the mind's imagined outcome?

There are some who sit on a podium selling you something you think you don't have. This is what the mego wants to see.

The mego wants confirmation that what it is lacking is actually present in somebody 'else' because it cannot be felt within. It 'looks' outwardly for nourishment because it has a palpable sense of inner absence and lack. The irony is, the only place you will ever find THIS is within you. You may sense a reflection of THIS in another, but in the end, it will come down to you. We are Awareness; it's just that the mego lacks the direct experience of THIS.

A person who sees WHAT-they-really-are does not necessarily conform to societal expectations, for they are no longer hypno-tised and misled by mental and emotional patterns or 'hooks'. They will not necessarily act to save face or follow certain ways that acquaintances or society expects of them. They are moved to act from the Heart Stream of Consciousness, and have surren-dered to what IS rather than being lost in the wandering imagi-nations of what could, should or might be.

To touch, glimpse or realise THIS, all you need do is *accept and let go*. Let go of all the attention grabbing thoughts in the way. You can. All it takes is for you to let go of what you are not. And if you do, you will not lose anything, but rather glimpse the One True SELF. You will feel and sense the aliveness in all things, in all people, in all life. You will touch the depths of the funda-mental Consciousness we *all* share. The paradox here is, THIS is yours, but you can never have it, for it is also everyone's and everywhere.

Letting go...

Letting go is an organic process born out of love and acceptance. In order to truly let go, do not attempt to force the issue, as that would be futile, for the addictive patterns will just repeat, repeat, repeat. Unlike the physical dimension, it is not a question of sheer brute strength. And neither does it mean fooling yourself by ignoring or hiding what arises in your mind. The way to really 'let go' is to develop the focus and attention to face and embrace what arises in your mind, for from this conscious Action comes resolution and freedom. Don't push negative, fearful or guilty thoughts away in an attempt to avoid them - simply give them your full attention. Watch them, but don't get caught up in them. You are not these thoughts, and you remain free to choose whether to 'run' with them or not. Observe them with the unbiased neutrality of full awareness. Watch and listen deeply to what is arising in your mind without judgement, for then those thoughts and addictions reveal their loving catalytic potential as true contributors to the realisation of THIS. In this sense, they are actually helpful tools. Once we accept and allow the pattern or thought to simply arise and be, we begin to sense from a deeper level of being, as we come out of the confines of the megoic 'head' and attune to the Heart Stream of Consciousness, wherein the answer or resolution naturally unfolds from Intelligent Love.

One example of THIS in worldly action can be found in the Bible. In the Sermon on the Mount, in Matthew 5:39 Jesus says: [39] *"But I say, do not resist such evil. If anyone strikes you on the right cheek, turn to them the other cheek also."*

And here's a very similar example from the Quran 41. [34]: *"The good deed and the evil deed cannot be equal. Repel the evil with one which is better, then verily he, between whom and you there was enmity, will become as though he was a close friend."*

Spiritual wisdom is ageless and without borders. The symbolism of turning the other cheek means far more than not retaliating – which in itself is an action contrary to antiquated societal expectations of what is considered to be a 'normal' response. Countering violence with the intelligent choice of non-violence is one thing, but when it arises from the core of one's being, and is then brought into the world, it is the actualisation of our innate Spirit; and the embodiment of THIS. A non-aggressive response from the 'victim' is at some point transformative for the 'doer' because it reflects the action back to the source of the problem. Because of the apparent lack of response, and the arising of spaciousness, at some point, the doer sees, feels and senses the ignorance of their actions reflected back at them. The stillness of a non-response acts like a mirror, allowing the doer to sense and feel the ineptitude of their aggression. Love attracts Love. Now I am not advocating how you should or shouldn't act, for you have the freedom to do as you see fit, all I am doing is commenting on how THIS may directly shape how we think, speak and act. Real forgiveness is not a thought, but the manifestation of Being.

A little word with unlimited spiritual power...

THIS is a remarkable little word, for at its deepest meaning is a key to Awareness.

THIS cannot learn or be taught anything. It has nothing to achieve or attain. The main reason you don't always see THIS (the ever-present Universal Awareness we *all* share) is because imprinted patterns held within the individual mind incessantly interrupt the permanent peace and beauty always here. A distorted, separate and somewhat superficial version of life (the mego) appears, covering the unchangeable Truth of *what-YOU-really-are*. But when you manage to stop and empty the commentary of the mind for long enough, THIS can be seen and acknowledged as *our* One unified Reality.

The core essential Awareness we all share is Consciousness without distinction. Ordinary unmodified Being. These words are simply clues or pointers and not the reality of THIS. At the root of life THIS is all you can ever truly be. To be anything 'else' without THIS present requires the imaginary dissection of a permanently unified Reality. In the anonymity of the One True SELF, the mego and all its burdens and pretence does not exist. When the mego is no longer the foreground of consciousness, it surrenders to the stillness of reality like a dying storm. Peace of Mind and Intelligent Love become increasingly apparent. For underneath the mego's concept of its own exclusivity, all is the

One True SELF.

Awareness is always here, always present. It *is* presence. Whether you recognise THIS is only ever down to how much the mego covers over that truth – for ultimately, there is no one 'else' or something 'other' to obstruct you. To imagine THIS doesn't exist or that you are separate from the Whole is a disjointed version of human consciousness. How can you be separate from everything that *IS*? Only the mego stops you from knowing THIS. In reality, the essential Oneness of THIS is ever-present, all-encompassing and inescapable. THIS does not 'exist', for it is existence itself.

In glimpsing THIS, we make ourselves available to Wholeness and Authenticity. For if we directly realise the basis of our unified relationship with one other, Nature and the Universe, then we will naturally live a life which exemplifies connection, balance and harmony. Act not for yourself alone, but for the Whole, for YOU are THIS!

2

∞ Mego & Personality ∞

Mego

The mego is individuated consciousness, the 'me' based fantasy of who you are; the ego of the distinct and separate 'me'. It is a fragmented identity, an archaic and outdated form of human consciousness wherein the individual mind imagines itself to be the epicentre of life.

The presence of the mego is not necessarily proven by witnessing how noisy and expressive someone is, but by it's self-pivotal nature, because it is always attempting to attract unwarranted attention and recognition. It is present in the loud or quiet, extrovert or introvert, for these are all ways and methods of attracting (or repelling) attention. Every mego wants to be appreciated, loved and fulfilled, so it seeks substitutes to replace that sense of lack according to its conditioning or *patterning*. The mego seeks what it thinks it lacks, introducing a multitude of substitutes to plug the gap it feels in consciousness.

Living your life indefinitely from the viewpoint of this partially sighted psychotic identity not only leads to addiction, depression, loneliness and separation, but it's also the mental barrier which prevents THIS from arising consciousness. We can't really say that THIS 'arises' for it is always here and now, but when the fractured identity of the mego is dropped, what underpins it has the 'space' to appear as the foreground of consciousness. So when we drop the mental commentary of the mego for long enough, we become present, because we revert to pure minded Awareness. THIS is the true meaning of presence.

Every mego is self-addicted to varying degrees. This can appear as an addiction to food, drugs, gambling, sex or alcohol, but many other forms also exist. Shopping, money, looks, gaming, texting, persistently worrying about the number of 'friends' or 'likes' one has on social media – opinions, criticisms, even work, exercise and so on. Work? Surely the act of work can't be a megoic addiction? Well it can be. For example, when driven by the goal of accumulating personal wealth so that the individual can establish power and control over others.

In the early part of the twenty-first century, materialism in all its 'forms' remains the most widespread addiction. Looks, money and possessions outweigh our essential spiritual values. The most common of these addictions to form is the mego's fervent belief that it's body-mind identity contains the absolute view of existence.

At the coreless core, YOU are THIS. THIS is what YOU essentially are. THIS is not a thought. Awareness is ONE, yours and mine, all of ours and none of ours, for having no personality or individual tendencies it is simply pure Consciousness, or Awareness itself. Consciousness and Awareness are pure Energy, the enlightened Reality present within each one of us. When you realise THIS, you will never be lonely again, for you will know that it is absolutely impossible to be alone. Only the mego can be lonely, for only the mego lives life from the fragmented perspective of separation. When all is realised to be the One True SELF, loneliness has no separate identity to cling to. There is no 'I' for THIS is One without any 'other'.

The mego sustains itself by clinging to separation, and in doing so thrives on distinction and constant comparisons of better and worse, greater and lesser, either/or, superior and inferior. The mego will do all it can to maintain the mirage of separation, for if it were to step aside and allow the anonymous THIS to naturally surface in your consciousness, it would be exposed as the isolated and incomplete identity it actually is. It would inevitably lose all power and become immersed in the Non-dual ocean of Awareness. So hold on tight, that's exactly what we're going to do.

The confined and confining mego exists as an illusory dam to the waters of unmodified Consciousness. That's why it's always under immense pressure; burdened to hold on, to perform, to prove itself, to continually strive for something 'other'. In the end, one way or another, the self-constructed dam of the mego will burst and be washed away by the waters of pure Consciousness, for in the end, THIS is all there is, all that is; *the Sole Cosmic Constant.*

The difference between the seeking restless mind of the mego and Awareness can be understood from looking at the way we perceive. A mind led by the mego looks out at the world from a viewpoint of separation so that any sense of identity comes from a distinction between the perceived subject and object – its motto could be *'seeing is believing'*. On the other hand, Awareness (which is ever-present and anonymous) has no requirement of object and subject, depends on nothing and yet remains ever-present and undeniably real – it is here and now before thought. It 'sees' in the sense that *it is seeing* itself.

Because we in the West are living in a materially driven society, the true focus and sacred value of life has been greatly overlooked or forgotten. The result is that most people delay looking deeply within and simply 'follow the herd' munching away on materialism, engaging multifarious mind-based addictions in order to fill their daily sense of lack. As we continue to live our lives in this dysfunctional way, our personal experiences, ideas, thoughts and emotions create a distinct route of false beliefs and addictions which the mego readily identifies with. This is individual patterning. So from conditioning, there arises a spiralling separation and a deeper identification with the mego. All of which makes us further removed from the Awareness of THIS (*what-YOU-really-are*).

It is challenging to look at oneself without favour or bias. But when life has repeatedly shown that you will not find lasting happiness in things, memories, projections, people or fleeting emotions, then you are ready to venture deep inside yourself to unveil the eternal Truth of *what-YOU-really-are*. Then a process of emptying, healing and spaciousness of the mind occurs as you increasingly recognise the coming and going of the mego. As you continue this 'emptying', a vibrant yet anonymous being-ness arises. It cannot be fully explained, other than by direct experience. Likewise, I cannot exactly reflect the direct experience of a warm breeze on my face, but I can use words to describe the sensation of it, but they are just words which attempt to describe, and being words they are not the living reality of the experience they point to. Words are not Awareness.

THIS is here and now, transpersonal, non-personal and never separate from *what-YOU-really-are*. Being neither a memory of the past or a projection of the future, it is always found within THIS moment. You cannot confine it or satisfactorily define it, other than to say it is what really *IS*, here and now. It is simply THIS, without division or manipulation.

Such is the paradox of the human being, for we cannot be divided from pure Consciousness. You may believe you are, but in truth you cannot be. For is the cloud separate from the stream? Is the ocean separate from the glacier? No they are all manifestations of the One water of Life.

The mego divides and restricts. It constantly preaches difference and separation when from the all-inclusiveness of Universal Awareness there is none. Of course bodies and minds are varied and different, but *what-YOU-really-are* is far more than all these. The Awareness YOU are underlies all forms and thoughts, and in the thought-free presence of that realisation, the individual dissolves in the Universal. You realise THIS. You see *what-YOU-really-are*. It's like a snowflake falling on the ocean. You melt into the Awareness of *our* essential Nature. A present intuitive knowing or knowingness arises, revealing that underneath the density of appearances, all is the One THIS. THIS is the fundamental dimension of Non-dual Being. It is the Divine Life-force itself, and the Sole Cosmic Constant.

Accepting that your mego is not the all-powerful single most important thing in the world can be a difficult, challenging and arduous task. All too often we tend to ignore what we feel inside, stating we don't have enough time, convincing ourselves we are too busy to be quiet and still. But if *what-YOU-really-are* is inherently at peace, still and aware, then who or what is proposing disconnection from THIS?

Don't kill the mego – love it to bits...

THIS is what *IS* when the mego caves in. The mego subsides not when it is killed, disowned or ostracised, but when it becomes enveloped by and merged with, the Peace and Love YOU essentially are. As your body is a temporary vehicle for *what-YOU-really-are,* so is the mind of mego. Then that understanding allows the observation of thoughts, memories and emotions to such a degree that the mego no longer dominates consciousness. It may arise, but it becomes increasingly recognisable. Would you not know if a doppelganger was claiming to be you?

So what is presently stopping you from seeing THIS? It's a very simple answer: the mego. For by imagining what you are, you are creating the biggest obstacle to that which you seek. So don't imagine or invent what you are. Sense *what-YOU-really-are.* Feel it within the depths of your being and follow it until it claims you as its own. When the mind gives up megoic illusions, you naturally reassume your innate connection with THIS. You surrender to the clear light of Consciousness, the Awareness of the One True SELF.

And how long will it take to see THIS? As long as you need. But it will only ever be possible here and now. How do you connect with the One True SELF? Doing your own work leads to the dropping of the thought that you are not the One True SELF. The question 'Am I the SELF?' does not arise when the doubting mind is purged. It simply IS. You are never separate from the

SELF – for THIS is *what* you already and always are.

When you have cleared enough space in consciousness, THIS will seemingly surface. When you have understood that nothing and nobody can give you what you seek, then the mind is reflected inward to the living reality of its ever-present core. That formless core is Love, Being, Truth, SELF, the Divine. THIS is *what* YOU are, where you come from, and all that *IS*. Whatever you do, whatever you say, THIS remains as it is. Unchanging and unchangeable it is the ever-present Awareness of the One True SELF.

Personality

The generally accepted notion appears to be that in order to find the One True SELF; we need to destroy the mego in order to be free. This is a belief. Many beliefs are false, partial or incomplete because they are biased hopes or personal assumptions and not direct experience. The One True SELF *is* Awareness itself. If you realise THIS – and remain open and available, then Authentic Doing manifests from Universal Being, and that is the most transformative and powerful Action that can take place in our world.

It is equally important to acknowledge our differences, to appreciate and celebrate individual gifts and skills. Be happy for another, not jealous, for in this way you are acting in harmony with the Heart Stream of Consciousness and contributing to the growth or expansion of human consciousness. Can you imagine a world without creativity and individual expression – a world without music, dance and laughter? It is through these, and many other deeply personal human experiences that something inexplicable and miraculous is shared.

Another belief of modern spirituality is that when conscious of the Awareness of the SELF, the personality remains ever-subdued or even destroyed. What takes place is that on merging with the universality of Awareness, the conditioned personality of the mego is experienced as being free of conditioning.

Awareness sees Awareness as the unified One. In the depths of the Non-dual experience the mind effectively becomes pure or disengaged, and there is no person, no thinker, and no doer whatsoever. It is simply THIS.

Following such a profound experience there will be the realisation of the sacredness of life and times of deep contemplation and stillness, but the opportunity for dancing, laughter and fun will remain. You will probably begin to laugh more, because you will begin to really recognise where a thought arises from, and find the dreamlike patterns of your mind increasingly comical and entertaining. You will begin to take yourself less seriously, and humility is a great leveller. Laughter is one sure way for everyone to glimpse their inherent freedom. For when we laugh, I mean *really* laugh, we let go of thought, and lose our-selves in the joy and freedom of THIS. It is in such times where we seem to 'lose' our-selves that we actually find the Universal and experience the joyous nature of existence. That's why laughter is a window to the direct experience of Being. Don't take my word for it, try it and see for yourself.

Realising THIS does not mean meeting expectations of onlookers by appearing a certain way, or copying the actions of another – but Authentically being *what-YOU-really-are*. A saint will be a Saint and a gardener will be a Gardener. Both still appear as individual personalities and unique characters. Both have the same organic life-values. Both will have realised *our* inner Awareness. In which case, thoughts of what to do and how to go about it arise from a wholistic interconnection with Universal Life, for consciousness is no longer led by the isolated mego.

The mind can remember and forget, whereas Awareness just infinitely *IS*. As Mark Twain wrote, 'If you tell the truth, you don't have to remember anything.' This suggests that being Authentic does not concern memory but living in harmony with the natural flow or presence of Life.

And how do you 'reconnect' to Awareness when you notice the negative thought patterns of the mego arising? As a form of practice, you can go back to the reality that THIS is *always* here now and ever-present. Sense the expansion of the space between Awareness and what is arising in your mind, and come back to THIS, come back to the Awareness YOU are. Watch the mind but don't think about it. Choose not to go into it, choose not to be distracted, and choose not to play along. Breathe. Come back to the present moment, where all is THIS, simply THIS. Breathe. Come back to the spaciousness that is the presence of Universal Life. Breathe. Watch but don't get dragged in. Breathe. Return to THIS.

The above is a simple exercise for the mind. In reality, you can never be separate from THIS, and questions of reconnection, disconnection and even connection do not arise. Being formless, there is nothing to hold on to. Being timeless, there is no future or past, for it is simply THIS.

Conscious evolution?

Awareness and persona go hand in hand. Not a conditioned personality, but an Authentic persona.

If you have integrated and grounded the direct experience of the SELF, then Authentic wholistic Action arises from a deep-rooted sense of interconnectedness and Oneness. Authentic Action arises from Awareness. On the other hand, action from the conditioned mego is pretty much always self-orientated, disconnected, biased and often harmful, whereas Action arising from the Heart Stream of Consciousness is healing, unifying and transpersonal. It is all-inclusive, and manifested through the realisation that all is essentially One. It is THIS which is the way to Change and transformation for humankind. If we can constantly put ourselves in another's shoes, then we will have a very good chance of embodying and sharing THIS.

New words and expressions are constantly evolving from

consciousness to support the embodiment of Awareness. This supports Authentic Change in our world. In order for such Change to take place, we must recognise, realise and actualise all that we are, for only then can we evolve into all that we may.

As Julian Huxley (1887-1975), the English evolutionary biologist once noted: *"The human species can, if it wishes, transcend itself — not just sporadically, an individual here in one way, an individual there in another way, but in its entirety, as humanity. We need a name for this new belief. Perhaps transhumanism will serve: man remaining man, but transcending himself, by realizing new possibilities of and for his human nature. "I believe in transhumanism": once there are enough people who can truly say that, the human species will be on the threshold of a new kind of existence, as different from ours as ours is from that of Peking man. It will at last be consciously fulfilling its real destiny."*

Some say there is no such thing as conscious evolution. Some say there is no need for Change, no choice, and nothing to be done. But how do you feel and what do you say?

3

∞ Thinking & Thoughts ∞

It may come as a bit of a shock, but you don't need to think to be *what-YOU-really-are*. Awareness is always here and now, so *what-YOU-really-are* is present before any thought. You just need to make room in your mind to see THIS, and the more space you unlock in your consciousness, the 'closer' you will come.

Let's take a look at the way in which we think. There is nothing wrong with unconditioned thought. For example, when looking at a beautiful sunset, the arising of the thought, 'This is a beautiful view', is obviously not problematic or detrimental to anyone, but beneficial and pleasurable. The problem lies in the conditioned thought and negative patterns which the mego addictively follows. The mego not only follows these patterns, it believes them to be absolutely true. In time, and with patience, the commentary of the mind will slow down and your consciousness will be more conducive to the stillness and space underlying thought. Then we can begin to watch our mind-patterns arising without blindly following them.

The accepted manner in which the mind operates in humans is incredible, astounding and amazing, and yet... flawed. This is because the way in which our Western logic operates is on a simplistic basis of either/or. For example, if I ask you to think of the word good, and then ask you to consider the opposing alternative – you will immediately dip into your mind and recognise it as being 'bad'. That's because we are conditioned into lateral Aristotelian thinking, a very handy tool for certain projects, but a mind-set which overlooks other answers, alternatives and unknown potentials.

The point I am making here is that when we think we are not complete, we presume the key to our completeness to be 'over there' or somewhere 'else'. If we seem lacking, we assume the opposite or 'other' to be full. In the 'spiritual' search this becomes a tool of rejection and confusion; from samsara to enlightenment, selfish and selfless, and so the list goes on. The consciousness of poles or *polaric thought* is so deeply entrenched in the human psyche that such opposites have become automatic presumptions. When present in our thoughts, feelings and emotions, they are the root cause of our inability to see the Whole and to engage life in a wholistic and Authentic way. Polaric thought can be helpful and beneficial in certain circumstances, yet it is only one way of thinking and not the only way. It is limited, and can be best understood as being a form of tunnel vision. In this sense, it is far from being a wholistic view. In the twenty-first century, the way in which we think as a species is dangerously out of date, so much so that we are close to becoming the next dinosaurs.

But there are windows when we naturally escape such ways of thinking and our mental conditioning. These are the times when love, joy, creativity and inspiration appear; when we are immersed in nature, or looking deep into the eyes of a baby, laughing your socks off (as we touched on in the previous chapter), contemplating beautiful works of art, rocking out to great music, making love – times when we touch a 'thought-free' freedom and glimpse beyond the confines of the mego. I suggest that what we are doing at these times is transcending the outdated way of the mind and engaging an intuitive expansive consciousness. These are the first shoots of Unividual being.

Looking at the 'my'

In order to glimpse the One True SELF, we need to peel back the outer layers of identity. One way you can do this is by looking at the 'my'. When we claim something as our own, then it becomes 'mine' and so we say 'my car' or 'my shoes' etc. – but these proclamations only reveal that anything followed by the word 'my' is just something that is sensed to be a belonging and not who or what you are.

Going deeper still, 'my thoughts', (the thoughts belonging to me) 'my mind' (the mind belonging to me) 'my ego' (the ego belonging to me) 'my consciousness' can all be seen to be the claimed belongings of a separate identity.

So who or rather what is it that all these apparent belongings belong to? When we see that every single possession that is described with the pronoun 'my' is purely a belonging and not the truth of *WHAT-we-really-are* then we are getting closer to THIS. You cannot say 'my THIS' – because THIS present moment belongs to all equally. It can never be yours and yours alone. Making THIS your belonging would be like saying 'my air I breathe'. The air we all breathe is not yours and yours alone. It is OURS. Yet you cannot see it or hold on to it. It simply *IS*. So it is with the One True SELF.

Seekers and Seeking

The idea of seeking is an interesting topic. Who is seeking and what are they seeking? In truth, the individual is seeking convergence with the Universal – for only then is the undeniable sense of peace and home alive in human consciousness. We could say that most people are 'seeking' to some degree.

Here's one way of looking at it. Let's imagine there are three types of seekers in the world:

1. Firstly, those who are seeking but remain unconscious of the fact they are seeking.
2. Secondly, there are those who imagine or believe they know what they are seeking, who strive to 'achieve' and who may appear to 'succeed', but at the height of their 'success' still find themselves surprisingly incomplete, because only then do they realise that they have not found what it is they were really looking for.
3. Thirdly, there are those who know they are seeking and

what they are seeking. And what is it that is being sought world over? It is Being, Truth, Awareness, Life, Source, God, Brahman, Reality, it is Spirit, and it is THIS.

THIS that is sought is not an object, it is not an idea, for you cannot see, think or imagine THIS. THIS is not found through holding on to details and beliefs, but by letting all of them go. Letting go of what the addictive mego conjures up. For when you no longer identify with the individual patterning, you find that you are still here, but in a more complete way than you could possibly imagine. In reality, THIS is more to do with the undoing of psycho-emotional patterns, and the mind revealing its own source rather than some outward seeking of something 'other'.

And yet, there is individual endeavour required to seek and find THIS, for as the Indian Sage Ramana Maharshi said:

No one succeeds without effort... Those who succeed owe their success to perseverance.

Consistently and relentlessly seek what is constant, for there you will find THIS.

Self-Enquiry

So, what is the most direct way to find or reach THIS inner truth? To go straight to the core, to delve deeply within, without predetermining what you will find. So, when you are ready, the most immediate and straightforward way of uncovering what YOU are, is to self-enquire. To ask yourself the question, 'Who am I?' – and for that internal process of discovery you ultimately need no tradition, no teacher and no teaching, just the courage and determination to continue no matter what inner conflicts and outer difficulties you come across.

So, as you read these words, ask yourself who is it that is reading. The mego's habitual answer is to reply, '*I* am reading' –

and to be happy to leave it at that. But who or what is the 'I' that knows it is reading? To find that answer, you will need to go beyond any notion of name, age, sex, colour, occupation, status, culture, nationality – and yes even beyond the idea that you are limited to a race called humanity. When you look for the source of this 'I' long and hard, you discover that it reverts back to the *primary thought* of existence, the 'I AM' – the primordial sense of being. However, if you were to transcend even that primary thought, then 'I AM' is seen to arise from the silent vibrant stillness of Awareness itself. For when there is no separation in consciousness, all is the One 'I'-less anonymous SELF.

Beyond 'I AM'

Awareness is not 'I' or 'I AM'. It is thought-free Reality present in every moment as THIS. Beyond all labels, thoughts and forms, Awareness is what YOU are. It is not a question of 'I' or 'I AM'. The idea that you will find your identity in Awareness is ambiguous. The present moment needs nothing to be. It is a mysterious wordless stillness. It has no specific or discriminating identity. It is already complete as it is. Awareness is un-owned aliveness, and simply THIS.

'I AM' arises as the initial sense-thought out of the anonymous Awareness of THIS. 'I AM' is the primary cerebral response or reaction to the experiencing of pure Consciousness. Without THIS, 'I AM' could not arise. 'I AM' is a comforter on the brink of THIS. 'I' as a person is duality. 'I' does not exist in the Non-duality of pure Consciousness. Nobody is present but presence itself. No 'I', no 'I AM', simply THIS.

Through this sacred Awareness, you are not denying that you exist, but realising your foundation and the foundation of *all life* to be indivisible, nameless and ONE. The primary thought of 'I AM' is transcended by the Divine vibrant stillness of THIS. That is why in realising THIS, even the primary identifying thought 'I AM' is left behind. For who is it that needs the 'I'? Only an 'I' needs the sense of an 'I'. THIS poses no question and asks for no response. Awareness is beyond any 'I'. Your core is Awareness itself, so your core is beyond identity. THIS does not require identity or thought. It is what permanently *IS*.

So what are you? YOU are Awareness itself. The appearance of any separate body, mind, emotion or idea is simply a layer, an outer covering. In the formless Heart of Being, there is nothing 'else' to be, for no 'else' or 'other' exists. To recognise THIS is your purpose, your reason for life, for it reveals the Peace of Mind and Intelligent Love YOU inherently are, and *all IS*. When you realise from direct experience that *what-YOU-really-are* is everything, there is no longer anything 'else' or 'other' to find.

Perhaps more crucially though, THIS holds the key to the survival of our race and our planet, for the way forward to a world of equality, peace and harmony will only ever be found from actualising THIS, and bringing THIS to life in the world. And it is here, for there is no other place for it to be found. THIS heavenly reality is not some idealistic future dream, but right here, right now, for it is the ever-present truth of what YOU are, what we *all* are. Recognising the timeless formless nature of Awareness is the only way to heal the world, because it is the One unifying Truth permeating and encompassing all life.

Any true and lasting change in global consciousness begins with you getting to know *what-YOU-really-are*. By getting to know the transcendent Reality of THIS. THIS is Awareness, available here and now without engaging or re-engaging the duality of the mind. Reality, Being, undisturbed Consciousness. It is the extraordinary ordinary. It is changeless, and yet it is the only true catalyst for Change. THIS is the revelation of *our* infinite loving and Divine Essence.

So, let go of the habits and patterns of the mego – and let THIS surface as the foreground of your consciousness. It's alright to do so. A star floating in the farthest depths of space is not clinging on, but being held and sustained by the Universal Intelligence of

THIS. Likewise, if you let go of the idea of who you think you are, what do you think will happen? That you will lose something? Or that you will come to an end? Perhaps you're worried that the world will forget the importance of who you are? It's safe to let go of all these things, for if you do so, you will discover that just like the stars and planets, you are nurtured and sustained by Divine Universal Intelligence itself. You are the One Life which can never be left. That's why THIS that YOU are can never feel lonely or unloved because it cannot deny itself. It is Whole, it is Intelligent Love, and it is ever-present.

Let go of all versions of who you are and what you believe Consciousness to be. Stop searching, stop seeking, for there is nothing to find. What YOU are here and now in the living serenity of THIS moment contains everything you need to know, for it is all. That's how infinite YOU are. If you know *what-YOU-really-are*, all concepts are seen to be temporary reflections of the mind and not THIS which just *IS*.

Direct Experience

YOU are Awareness. The Awareness of the SELF is *what-YOU-really-are*. How deep and lasting that recognition is – will be drawn from the direct experience of the dissolution of the mego in Awareness. A direct experience as Awareness delivers a profound and undeniable knowingness. Not a time-based learning in a conceptual sense, but the immediate actuality of non-conceptual Being. It's not that it suddenly dawns on you, or that you 'get it' – but more that you are overwhelmed by the One inseparable ocean of Life. The little you at its core is revealed to be the One eternal ocean of Awareness. The doubting, inquisitive mind is still and silent, allowing a direct experience of pure Consciousness which is Universal, timeless and infinite.

Words are not the direct experience, that is they fall short of capturing it, for the direct experience of the One True SELF-Awareness-Brahman cannot be fully explained in words. You cannot grasp it; for there is no-thing to grasp. It is beyond thought. Words only act as a reference to the direct experience, for they are not the actual experience they refer to. They are recreations which simply point and share, without proving and defining. For example, I could explain the smell and taste of an apple to you, but if you had never eaten an apple before, the act of you smelling and tasting the apple yourself would provide you with the direct experience of that apple. Then you would need no explanation.

THIS is the direct experience of Awareness. With the mind stripped bare, Awareness is revealed as the One fundamental Reality. THIS is only available to you and you alone, for it cannot be copied. And yet you can never have it, never own it. For when you experience dissolution in Awareness, there is no you here to identify with the experience.

What-YOU-really-are...

Who you think you are may be many things, a face, a name, a father, a mother, a plumber, and so forth. *What* YOU are is THIS. But it's not yours alone. For the THIS that is you – is the THIS that is me. They are formless and inseparable. It is not personal. It is not an identity. There is no 'I' in Awareness. When you're finally ready to give up the idea of *your* separateness and *your* specialness, then you are ready to find the anonymous peace of THIS. When you find THIS, you will immerse in the One True SELF which everyone and everything already and always *IS*.

THIS expresses the unchangeable timeless and true. It is not a thought or a form which can be adapted to personal opinion or altered to fit. YOU are THIS, and yet you cannot grasp what THIS is. When we drop the 'I' and uncover Awareness, there is only THIS. If there is only one complete presence and no sense of any 'other', would an 'I' need to arise at all? Essence, SELF, Truth is not an individual seeking an identity, but the THIS-ness of formless Being itself.

The 'I-less' nature of Reality

When you dissolve into THIS, there is no 'I' to be found, because no 'I' is needed. No distinction or comparison is required or made without the arising of separation. So when you are fully absorbed in the Universal inseparability of Awareness, no question or doubt needs asking or answering. YOU are THIS. THIS is what YOU are. Nothing is needed – for everything and nothing is absolutely present. There is just THIS. Awareness requires nothing because it always *IS*.

Perhaps you may be worried that by accepting the possibility of surrendering to THIS you will lose your individuality, your character, your power? That you will become some sort of mindless zombie? The truth is that you will lose nothing from the act of surrender, but as a consequence of THIS, life will be lived from the Heart Stream of Consciousness and not from the isolated wants and desires of the disconnected mego. Of course you will continue to do things, but behind any doing, you will be led, steered and nourished by the Intelligence of Life itself. And how will you be led? You will be led by surrendering to what *IS*. By no longer depending on old patterns and distorted or biased memories to define what is happening or about to occur. What is here and now when there is no 'me' in the driving seat? THIS – only THIS. Nothing needs adding, nothing needs taking away. THIS is Reality without the meddling mego, without the fractured individual mind of separation.

THIS is here...

Why alter what is whole and complete in order to find what is whole and complete? Why would anyone want to do that? The division of consciousness occurs when the old animalistic fear of not having enough and wanting more continues, because the individual identity has not grounded in Wholeness. The mego is a transient fractured identity brought about by a self-absorbed version of consciousness. This is known to be true because the mego cannot 'see' THIS – but the Awareness of THIS can 'see' the mego for exactly what it is.

The mego appears through the reliance on concepts such as fear, distinction, separation and division, in fact anything which separates, fractures and isolates. Even the senses we know so well propose that the subject ('I') and the object ('that') of duality is the absolute reality. But behind all perception is the Awareness of THIS. All life is moving towards recognising, realising and establishing THIS. What we call evolution is really only THIS becoming aware of itself in human consciousness; THIS becoming increasingly apparent, THIS gradual flowering of consciousness here on Earth.

4

∞ Why THIS? ∞

The Truth of Life is only found in THIS moment...

A small word with a powerful underlying meaning, THIS is a tool, a key for freeing consciousness from the control of the mego. There are several reasons for the transformational power of the little word THIS:

1. When used as an all-inclusive description of pure Consciousness, it refers to the totality without division or separation.

2. The word THIS, when used as an expression of all-inclusivity, automatically takes you out of the old polaric thought of the mind, and points to the infinite expanse of pure Consciousness.

3. It provides a precise Non-dual indication of Awareness *without* requiring analysis or description.

4. It clearly reflects what *IS* when subject and object dissolve – what anonymously remains when the mego is transcended.

5. When used as an all-encompassing description, it nullifies the subject-object of duality.

6. It is a non-discriminating sharing of pure Awareness.

7. It requires no 'other' word or addition to reveal itself. THIS.

8. Used as an expression of what *IS*, it is always here and now, always THIS.

9. In this sense it is *not* a contradistinction or pointing to a separate distinct other, – but Universal presence.

10. Used alone, without preceding a noun, and not as a precision or emphasis – it is complete, unified and whole. Just THIS, only THIS, simply THIS.

The window to the Truth of what YOU are is found in the Awareness of the present moment. How is that present moment most often described and interpreted? Answer: THIS moment. THIS cannot be found in the past or the future, in that, then or when, but always here and now whatever the apparent consequences. That's why your memories are not YOU and your future hopes and dreams cannot be YOU. THIS *is what-YOU-really-are* because it is unconditioned aliveness right here, right now. Being anonymous, it is transpersonal Being and the unmodified Consciousness of the One True SELF.

Secondly, the word THIS is not being used to denote a certain perception or a specific identity, as in *this* house or *this* idea, but as a way of describing the ever-present indivisible Whole. Within THIS everything is. Without THIS nothing is. THIS is behind, within and beyond all that is seen and unseen. When you are asleep – you are THIS, when you are dreaming – you are THIS and when you are awake – you are THIS. When you let go of the confined and restricted idea of the individual self, you find THIS, because THIS is not *a* person, but transpersonal 'I-less' Awareness.

In the still calm Awareness of the SELF, the once chattering 'you' is absorbed. You merge with the still, vibrant Source. The 'I-dentity' that was once the focal point of individual consciousness is no longer present, because YOU are realised to be anonymous. THIS is the mego-less dimension of non-distinction, unchanging, all-inclusive and permanently Whole. Needing nothing, wanting nothing, requiring nothing yet existing before, within and beyond everything. It is unconfined and beyond the capacity of the mind to pin down. To hold onto THIS would be like trying to grab a handful of air, which YOU already have and are.

So the little word THIS is illogical, paradoxical and about as close to Truth as words can bring you, and yet it mirrors the coreless core of Awareness. Boundless and endless yet always here it is the everlasting Infinite. If you spend your life trying to mentally grasp and understand THIS, then you will never find and live it. It is not an idea or a concept you can get your head around. Neither can you argue THIS. It is not a topic or belief which can be debated. You cannot understand THIS, you simply need to *be* what YOU already and always are in Authentic Abundance.

Revealed through an inquiry into your own inner spaciousness, it is not for anyone to discover in you, but for you to recognise and actualise. And yet you cannot find or keep THIS. You cannot buy or sell THIS. You cannot hear or not 'hear' THIS. You cannot touch or not 'touch' THIS. You cannot see THIS or fail to 'see' THIS. For it underlies, permeates and transcends all of these. It has no value, yet it is life's greatest treasure. It has no meaning and yet is beyond all knowledge. In truth, THIS doesn't *need* to be realised or not realised, for it is here, now, and always YOU.

So, forget about seeking. Ultimately, seeking only stands in the way of THIS which YOU already and always are. You were THIS yesterday, are THIS today and will be THIS tomorrow. THIS is the timeless indivisible dimension of Being YOU always are. When YOU are THIS, all separation has gone. Time and space no longer confine. There is no coming and going, no to-ing and fro-ing. There is just THIS that YOU are, the all-encompassing Awareness of the SELF which simply *IS*.

Your habitual mego acts like a shadow in front of the sun, like curtains covering a window. To let the light in, you must let go of the mego's belief in separation – which is what stands in the way. Do your work, draw back, remove your confined sense of self and let the Universe Be. Let the light in. Then it will be clear that *what*-YOU-really-are is THIS light.

Time is the great conditioner. Our minds run backwards and forwards, but when you are fundamentally present, then time is rendered powerless. It is transcended along with matter and space. THIS exists within and beyond. As YOU are THIS, then *what-YOU-really-are* exists beyond time, and is timeless. As THIS exists without depending on form, then the ultimate truth of what YOU are exists beyond form, so it is true to say that YOU are formless. Incredible as it may sound, *what-YOU-really-are* goes beyond thought, matter, time and space.

THIS is not an idea, but Reality. With the 'I' present, THIS *IS*. Without the 'I' present, THIS *IS*. Without ideas and idiosyncrasies, THIS *IS*. The eternal YOU is not some-thing or some-one that lives forever, but pure Consciousness. It was never born and can never die. It is Life itself. Life goes beyond birth and death, beyond any idea or thought of what it is, because it is not confined to mind, space, time or matter.

THIS and That...

If what you are lacking and trying to find is pointed to or described to as *That*, then it suggests you are presently separated from what you seek. You will be separate from it if you are seeking for it, because you have already identified with the idea that it is not here. But you can never be divided from what you are trying to find, because *what-YOU-really-are* is the ever-present, all-inclusive THIS. A fractured or individual consciousness is the only obstacle to THIS. It is only the mind's patterning which proposes something is missing, and the way forward is hard and complicated. THIS is simple and effortless. It is *what-YOU-really-are* without trying to be, for it is *our* essential Being.

When you look into the depths of the present moment you will see that subject and object are One. They simply fuse together. Any conceptualisation of difference vanishes. How can this be? It means that what is behind both the subject and the object must share the same Source, the same indivisible Reality. What you are looking at – is unquestionably known to be indivisible from *what-YOU-really-are*. When all labels of what you are experiencing are put to one side, all that can be seen is THIS. In Essence YOU are THIS, for there is nothing 'else' to be.

It is the mego which dissects the unified reality of Consciousness. So it is your own mind of separation which holds you back from recognising the Oneness of THIS. The choice is always yours. You don't have to live your life continuously divided from *what-YOU-really-are*. When the divisive mego is quietened and stilled, you become increasingly available to glimpse the Oneness of Life itself. The Whole without any parts.

THIS is not a commodity belonging to a person. It cannot be defined by names and labels. When all people and all things are no more, THIS will still be. It has always been. Nothing can stop it from being, for it is Being itself.

When you open your eyes and look out at the world, before you begin thinking and dissecting what you see and apportioning names and labels, then THIS is all you truly see. YOU are THIS without a subject and object. When Awareness meets Awareness, then all is One. In reality it cannot be anything else. It cannot be seen elsewhere. It is right here, right now. Free from the personal identification and the meddling mind of the divisive mego, all that remains is THIS.

THIS underlies and inhabits your waking, dreaming, sleeping, thought, breath, body, mind, soul. The same unified Reality that underlies anyone or anything else. It is not yours or ours, for it cannot belong, it is not a belonging. It is the timeless presence which underlies all that *IS*, the pure Energy Consciousness of existence. The THIS-ness. The more you try to name it, label it, and define it, then the more you lose its meaning. Yet here it is present in THIS very moment, untouched by thought, not belonging to anyone or anything, simply Being. And if you call THIS nothing, then all is nothing.

There are no words which can truly convey THIS, because it cannot be grasped by the logic of the intellect. Words are only used to share and express THIS. In a strange illogical way, it is the space and stillness they introduce which shares a real transformative power. Like the breath, that space behind the words allows them to be spoken and heard – and their true meaning to be contemplated. The little and seemingly insignificant word THIS is a sacred link, a portal between physical existence and *our* 'spiritual' Reality.

And simple it is. Why is it simple? Because only following the mind of mego makes it out to be complicated. THIS is eternally present without seeking, knowing or needing to know. So get rid of the idea that THIS is complicated, in fact let go of any notion of what it is at all. If you hold a definitive and fixed opinion of what THIS is, then it is not THIS.

THIS is not yours...

The One True SELF is not yours. We are in it and it is within us without distinction. Forget the idea of finding *your* True SELF. What you are looking for is not yours alone but Truth itself. That's why it may be called the One True SELF. Looking at a tree, the sky, another person, in essence it sees itself. There is no difference whatsoever. Human consciousness has used the physical senses to go beyond them, and in doing so, separation melts into pure Consciousness. All is realised to be One. All people are seen to be enlightened Awareness at their core. Life is the One Consciousness. When the limited idea of form is transcended, then the limitless dimension of Being appears.

So everything is THIS. Everything you can't see is THIS. If you can't see THIS, then you are missing the essential Truth of *what-YOU-really-are*. If you glimpse THIS then let go of the idea – and live what remains.

Life without THIS...?

Life without THIS will never be satisfied and whole, simply a masquerade, a partial existence that will create cycles of suffering in you and those around you. You know that to cause suffering to another creates guilt and suffering in you; but why is that? It's not about laws, morals and religious codes, but something more fundamental. When you cause suffering to another, then you suffer too because you are in conflict with the unified Reality of Being. You are in effect, hurting yourself. So why hurt yourself? Only someone who is disconnected from the loving Intelligence of Life would do that.

Life without THIS Awareness is the world of mego. In that psychotic madness, money would be God, and people would become increasingly cut off from each other. Technology would be used to speed up the sense of separation, causing people to constantly compare their looks and contrary views rather than using it to find lasting connecting values and global solutions. In the world of mego, quality would be on the decline, and the planet would be governed by those who had the most rather than any real sense of sharing, equality and democracy.

The world of mego would be a world of division and spiralling poverty. The rich would become richer and the poor poorer. Natural cataclysm would rapidly increase owing to the mindless stripping of the Earth's resources for financial gain, and war would be a constant battle.

Is this the type of global society you'd like to live in? Well you already are. This is what our world is like in 2015. Now what are you going to do about it? Are you simply going to say all we need to do is 'love life' while greed, war, disease and religion tear humankind and our planet to pieces?

Or do you choose the possibility of Authentic Change through the Action of Love?

Are you prepared to rise up and be counted?

If you are, then THIS is the open-ended answer.

5

∞ THIS Mountain of Awareness ∞

Even if we end up wiping ourselves off the face of the planet, THIS will still be here. THIS is always here. Embracing and integrating THIS remains the only way of stopping all the madness, violence and insanity which is currently destroying our world. Throughout history, humanity has undergone peaks and troughs in consciousness which have fundamentally altered the way we think and act. What we are going through at this time in human history is an opportunity, a window for Change. That's Change with a capital 'C' because it's Authentic, and for the Whole.

The process of life is an awakening journey, a priceless opportunity to reveal the living truth of *what-YOU-really-are,* and the way in which THIS is made alive in the world. THIS is the only way Spirit becomes embodied in human consciousness, for THIS is the One True Spirit.

Imagine that life is a mountain that you climb over time. At the peak of the mountain there is a bright beacon of golden light, an infinite light radiating out across the valleys below. The light would remain unchanged through the passing of time, always there, always alight, the eternal THIS. The light would reach everywhere, but you would only see THIS if your senses permitted, or rather you were open and available seeing THIS. Sometimes you would feel or sense its warm glow and not see it. Imagine the light's warm sun-like rays gently caressing your face, and imagine that you were only able to see just a few feet ahead. You would feel the warmth of the light and not know its origin, but nevertheless you would know the light to be here and Real.

As the mountain symbolises the path of life, then what

controls the weather conditions that can hinder or help your view of the light? How you think, speak and act determines the possibility of seeing or sensing THIS light from absolutely anywhere. Your consciousness and the dense patterns it holds or doesn't hold is the key factor, for the only barrier to the light is the density of your own thoughts. You may not be able to see and feel the light directly for long undisturbed periods of time, but you can experience its reality from wherever you are on the mountain.

In this way we can comprehend that what was revealed by Lao Tzu, Buddha, Guru Nanak, Jesus or Mohammed is relative to the path they travelled up the mountain. What angle, position and view they attained at different times defined their explanation of the light. As they approached the Light, the message would become more attuned to the Love and Peace radiating from its core. For instance, standing at the bottom of the valley, one's view of the light at the summit would exist, but would not be as clear or as defined as the feel or view of someone stood half way up the mountain; for the greater the distance between the person and the Source – the less warmth, and the greater the chance of other 'things' getting in the way, leading to a more vague interpretation. The sort of things that could get in the way would be the distracting thoughts in your head, because your attention cannot be in two places at once. To really see the light you would need a still mind in order to focus on it.

The closer to the zenith these spiritual explorers came, the clearer the message and the greater the transformational content of what they shared. *They all* carried varying degrees or versions of truth, truths which were coloured by their own cultural roots. *They all* accessed a transcending consciousness beyond the mego which they explained and shared according to their path, position or viewpoint on the mountain. The explanations they each gave for the way in which they received that information were varied, but the underlying Source of the loving intelligence they perceived was One and the same. This is why no single religion holds the sole or absolute truth, and yet THIS is the foundation of all Authentic religions. Their teachings appear unique and separate owing to factors such as their era, culture, and the character and capability of the messenger to convey the message. And yet there is a golden thread of Truth running through them all. All Authentic religions and philosophies arise from THIS, for it is *their* primordial formless form, sole origin and *what-YOU-really-are.*

On such a mountain, in Reality everyone would be able to see the light, so everyone would be in touch with the light of Awareness whether they knew it or not. To physically turn away or to approach the light would be your own decision, so any ability to 'see' would correspond directly with freewill and not the physical senses alone. As you approached the light, the more warmth you would feel and the greater effect it would have on you. The closer you came to the brightness of the light, the greater its intensity, and the more you would be drawn to it, like a moth to a flame.

If you are standing within a busy hustling crowd on the mountainside then your view may well be restricted by the actions, movements or mental and emotional noise of others. So giving your-self a little space, and finding a better view will help you. You might climb to the top of a tree, for then you will not to have to rely on the experiences of others, or the hearsay of the crowd around you, and you will be looking and seeing for yourself.

A crowd may gather anywhere on the mountainside, and could mislead themselves and others into believing they were the only ones who really knew about the light, or they were the only ones who owned the book of the light. This wanting to own what is naturally everyone's would make the experience and knowledge of the light a matter of secondary importance because opinions, thoughts and debate would never reach the direct experience of the light. When you see the Light, you would know, for you would be the light.

Standing in the light you would instinctively be aware there was only One undivided Reality and that each group or individual was simply inventing and interpreting their own separate understanding of a greater all-inclusive whole. And without seeking the direct experience of the light, people would endlessly seek in the mind of thought, theory and logic for something that was there, overshadowing them all at the top of the mountain.

So, if you find your view blocked by your thoughts, words and deeds or the knock-on effects of the actions of those around you, then in order to get a glimpse of the light, you will need to climb up on a rock or a tree to be able to gain an unobstructed view. Sometimes the mystery of life will create this very possibility, appearing as if by chance. From the varied experiences that we encounter on the path of life we will undoubtedly come across what are considered 'positive' and 'negative' experiences, but all experiences whether perceived as 'good' or 'bad' serve to provide us with an opportunity to recognise more of that light. Sometimes it's good to be alone on the mountainside, for then, when the mind eventually drops away, the rays become obvious, and you will laugh in wonder as to how you didn't see them before.

If you were standing close to the light, you would see that all life was a part of the same interwoven Whole. You would have an undeniable knowingness that all was One. It wouldn't be a thought or an idea, but a powerful certitude from within. You would see that each individual was a living example of the potentials of human existence. You would also see that together, we have the ability and power to Act *en masse*, to consciously evolve as a race.

We tend to see our state of existence as one that still has the mountain to climb – but what if our fundamental state of being was inseparable from the golden light – and that once we stilled our minds enough, our universal core was recognised to be THIS sacred essence?

Then you would not just get close to the light, but enter the light. Should you do so, the you that entered the light will be gone forever. Then all would be seen as THIS, and no thought or emotion would arise. There would be no you for it to arise from or to. THIS is the Truth of Non-duality, the stillness, the silence, wherein no thoughts arise, wherein nothing is needed, no doing is required and Life simply IS.

And do not be conformed to this world, but be transformed by the renewing of your mind...
– Romans 12:2

At some point, you might hear the cry of your small child, and be pulled out of the infinite glowing warmth and back onto the far side of the mountainside. You are changed. Your mind is renewed. You have found that YOU are THIS light, you are inseparable from THIS light, and now THIS light is not only alive within you but the aliveness in everyone and everything. A transformation of consciousness has taken place and the individual has dissolved in the Universal, changing their consciousness forever. There is no going back; there is now just THIS experience of the mountain and the light simultaneously. Wherever you find yourself on the mountainside, the light is known to be there as well, for it is carried within and seen everywhere. Not as a memory, but as a knowingness beyond thought. There is no clinging to the idea or memory of the light, for the light has transformed your mego consciousness. Once you have accepted and grounded THIS in your consciousness, you are free to be the universally led Individual.

If THIS transformation takes place across the world, then a new wholistic consciousness will manifest. THIS consciousness would naturally establish a 'new' framework of living and a 'new' pathway for global society. THIS consciousness would appreciate all that has passed, acting openly and creatively in such a way that 'progress' would be a unified reality. The good of the Whole would be the common and binding factor, as each person would understand themselves to be a unique part of that same indivisible Whole.

THIS consciousness would encourage sharing and participation. No opinion would be more valuable, and no Unividual more or less important than another. Values, codes and ethics would be inherently common to all. Each Unividual would be living their Authentic role, and being aware of their Wholeness, would be naturally connected to the principles of resolution, love and peace. THIS would be the way to really live – not *the* final answer, but an Authentic evolving way of living which would return us to the harmonious natural ways we have overlooked or forgotten.

Returning to the mountain, we can see that each individual has a 'view' of what constitutes reality. These 'views' are all reflections and interpretations of a greater Whole. Jesus, Mohammed, Krishna, Lao Tzu, Guru Nanak, Zoroaster and others all had differing ways of telling the same story – because it came from taking their unique journey up the very same mountainside and sharing their realisation of the One light. They were born in different places, into differing cultures and religions and into varied social strata of society, and yet they all provide the same clues to THIS at the heart of their teachings.

These and many other pioneers of consciousness all revealed clues to *our* human potential. We are now in an age where the exploration of *our* spiritual potential is being undertaken by growing numbers. Day by day people are waking up and realising that the present megoic society is doomed. It is unable to express and sustain the qualities of Being which nurture *our* wholistic health and well-being, and it falls way short of inspiring and enlightening the Soul. We have gone past the time when we simply accepted '...*something is rotten in the state of Denmark*' as Marcellus said in Shakespeare's Hamlet. That time of turning a blind eye to what is going on throughout our world is ending. THIS is the time to stand and deliver the Action and Change that will benefit the Whole. You are the Action. You are the Change. You are THIS.

Any form of consciousness which is Authentically grounded in a human being has the potential to be utilised by *all* others. What these 'spiritual' explorers gave us was the opportunity to perceive the fundamental Reality of SELF, Awareness, or Being. Their Authentic interpretation of THIS in the world came about by them letting go of duality, and of Non-duality too. They were Authentic Souls naturally contributing to the Whole in their own, unique way. They were all revolutionaries, heretics or outcasts to varying degrees. It seems that we are more likely to find these truths being expressed by a person who contravenes the standard accepted beliefs and 'spiritual' understandings of the time. They lived from experience and knowledge, rather than from intellectually regurgitating a half-baked truth, for *Chinese Whispers* always end up distorted, and the true meaning of the original statement only becomes lost in the wandering minds of others.

Wholeness manifests in the world through Change and Action. The Wholeness of Unividuality comes not from the individual realisation of the Universal, but from the grounding and organic integration of the Universal in the Individual. That's Individual with a capital 'I' because from the mego diving into Awareness, the Non-dual Acts in the world through the necessity of the dual. The wonder of human existence is that in our lifetimes we can uncover THIS Wholeness and be a conscious contributor to Life while at the same time benefiting from it too. Contribution *is* benefit. Giving *is* receiving when you realise Wholeness. Wholeness gives value, belonging, meaning, positivity, creativity and knowingness. The arrival of Wholeness *en masse* signifies we are at a point in human evolution when we can observe and integrate the multilayered aspects of THIS.

Belief systems have played an important defining role in the structure of society, but today we need to redefine and evolve these structures and teachings, to look at the deeper truths that connect *all* faiths. In this way humanity will be able to walk the path of our true nature, the path of unification.

Each one of us knows that life is essentially good, that the highest potential reality we can perceive is one where love, peace and harmony are present. This *'Garden of Eden'* is not some childlike optimism or unreachable ideal of a deluded dreamer, but the very essence and Heart of what we are, what THIS is. Consciousness unobstructed by the senses *is* heaven on Earth. We have all experienced THIS fundamental Being-ness at some point in our lives, which is why we sense it as being founded in reality. Indeed, THIS is 'happening' all the time. However, the sense of connection may have only appeared for a split second or two. And yet the paradox is because it's here and now, we don't even need to remember. It is simply our natural way of being.

6

∞ You Can't Touch THIS! ∞

The Infinite THIS...

THIS cannot be altered, rearranged or disturbed by anyone or anything. Beyond time and space it is the transcendental dimension of Being, the all-encompassing un-manifest reality of Spirit. Ever-present, it is glimpsed when the mego no longer obstructs *our* pure-minded Nature. As we already know, the mego gets in the way by dividing consciousness from its organic Wholeness – in other words you fool yourself into believing that the mego is the complete truth of who you are, when it is not. This unconscious assumption is similar to having the belief that the true core of a peach is its hard 'stone'. But if we look further still, right inside the 'stone' – there is a seed, which is alive and just waiting for the opportunity to share itself in the world. And how would you get to know about the seed which lies at the core? By not assuming things to be a certain way and by taking a look deep inside. We look when we are ready to look, and not before.

Human beings can wipe each other out and gradually destroy the planet in the process, but we can't touch THIS. MC Hammer really was right! THIS can be realised but it cannot be reshaped or personalised. That would be like pointing to the space in front of you and saying 'don't anyone else breathe this air in front of me, because it's mine'. So ludicrous and childlike is the little mind of mego, it is becoming outgrown through the evolution of human consciousness. The spoilt child of humanity is being made to grow up. Getting ready to leave the nest and take on individual, global and universal responsibility. If we do not all stand up to be counted, the world as we know it will face the consequences of our ignorant actions. If this scenario does occur, it will be due to the global failure of humanity to act in alignment and accordance with the Heart Stream of Consciousness and the light of Awareness *we all* share.

THIS cannot be separated or apportioned. It cannot be divided. Truth is Truth. You know the Truth when you see it, feel it or read it. How do you know? Because it is what YOU are. You cannot deny THIS once you have uncovered your Naked Being-ness. There is no choice, no debate as to the reality and validity of THIS. You cannot decide how it is or how it should be. Do you think that a leaf orders the wind where to blow it to or that nature is somehow lacking something?

You are exactly where you need to be now. You are where you presently are because of the lessons you need to learn and the gifts you are able to share. We are on Earth to live, love and learn. But if you drop all discriminating notions of difference and separation, and *be* what you are, you will be aligned with the Consciousness of Life, the pure Mind of the Universe. To be True to Life simply requires the complete and unconditional surrender to THIS that YOU already are. To accept that whatever takes place in this moment is okay and holding the awareness of not getting emotionally caught up in events. Don't take life so personally. Life is Universal. Things don't happen to *you*, they just happen. Life's not personal so don't be offended. There is a greater meaning and purpose to what takes place in your life than the mego can see. Anything that occurs isn't really about you; it's just how it *IS*. Accept it. It's that way for a reason. In the wisdom of acceptance, you may live unconditionally, accepting whatever occurs without becoming personally identified with it. And rest assured you are here for a very good reason.

You are not driving the car of life. The idea that you are the driver is the big illusion of the mego. If you let go of the idea that you are the driver, you will discover that you did not need to be the driver in the first place; that the accidents of your life were because you sometimes chose and attempted to go the wrong way up a one-way street, got lost, went too fast or too slow, or that you became frustrated when you couldn't get the motor going. The only notion that you were driving came about from an isolated sense of being. When separation steps aside, then what is truly conscious right here, right now takes control. The driving force of your life becomes the Intelligence of Life itself.

To describe THIS definitively and conceptually would be an attempt to confine what may not be confined. Yet throughout history, THIS has been repeatedly witnessed. So exactly what is the residual evidence of THIS? Well, perhaps the perfume of Love and Peace, the trail of humility and the recognition of equality and Oneness are clues which lay scattered throughout the path of our history. Rather like the fragrance of a beautiful flower, the scent still remains, and although this is not the flower itself it allows us to somehow reconnect with THIS deeper joy.

Peace, stillness, joy, inspiration and love – these are qualities of Awareness. These same qualities or properties are found within all ancient wisdom teachings, teachings which continue to profoundly affect us not because they express personal opinions, but because they share transpersonal Wisdom. In the most profound examples of the sharing of Universal Wisdom, the welfare of others is consistently placed above any idea of prioritising the mego self. Why was this? Because they realised they were inseparable from THIS that *all* are. We are all One.

That's why THIS cannot be touched. At the core of your being, YOU are THIS Buddha was describing. The same THIS Jesus conveyed. The indescribable THIS Lao Tzu shared. The infinitely named THIS found at the root of Sikhism. THIS ever-present unchanging Reality of Brahman.

THIS is *our* I-less eternal Nature, and Reality itself. To think that you have to be like, unlike or dislike any of these individuals or their beliefs is your downfall. You do not need to think to be THIS. THIS is what YOU are beyond any imagined thought. It is your natural way of being. It is Being. So surrender, drop all ideas of what THIS is, for then you will be able to be conscious of it; for THIS is *what-YOU-really-are*.

All religions and wisdom teachings ultimately lead you to THIS. Not so you could become another means of further dividing humanity, but quite the opposite. THIS is within all beliefs and non-beliefs; Muslim, Christian, Hindu, Buddhist and Atheist, yet THIS requires none of them in order to be. It is what is, what was and what will be, the timeless Reality. Unrestricted by the confines of time and space, THIS was here before belief systems were conceived and will be here long after they have all gone. It is always HERE. It is the Sole Cosmic Constant. Ideas of THIS come and go in the world but THIS remains within and beyond any idea. So again, you see MC Hammer really was right... you can't touch THIS!

To assume one group are *the* chosen people or that a nation is *the* greatest nation in the world is no different from the idea of *a* unique son of God. All such ideas feed separation, and are partial truths at best. The Truth is all-inclusive, and the Whole is the Truth. Not one side, one view or one belief. Any such notions are guaranteed to escalate separation, and separation is undeniably the work of the mego.

The mystery of *what-YOU-really-are* is pure Awareness. That's why you can never absolutely equate *who* you are with non-personal Awareness. 'Who' does not exist in Awareness. You are a human being and although you can realise your interconnected relationship with Awareness, it can never be *your* personal identity. THIS is not personal. THIS is all-inclusive 'I-less' Awareness. Awareness is the coreless core of yourself and *all* others, so it can never be yours. And as all is One, which is the living Reality of pure Awareness, then no 'I' is needed or required. That's why Awareness is what-YOU-really-are, and not who. And yet there is an Authentic You interconnected with the Whole.

The truth of what you are cannot be confined to any particular shape or form. It doesn't need to claim anything, for it is within and beyond all these things. THIS cannot be cut up and divided. In whatever way you try to divide it, you cannot. To attempt to do so would be like trying to cut up an endless ocean with a pair of scissors. You might feel that you have done it, because you went through the motions of cutting with the scissors and saw the water move, but in the end you have achieved nothing. Your actions were pointless. All you've done is temporarily disturb the appearance of the ocean. Afterwards the ocean is as it was. Whether you acted or not, THIS remains unchanged.

Anyway, why would you want to rearrange, alter or disturb THIS? Only the divisive mind of mego would act in that way. Of course any such action is fruitless. The self-centred mego cannot change the ever-present all-permeating Intelligent Nature of the Universe. You cannot alter the way THIS is. So there are only two options. You can get in the way or get in the flow. By getting in the way you create suffering, turmoil and unrest for yourself and others. Even when you have grabbed all the desires and attainments you can, and gathered all the rewards the world can offer you, you will still be lacking. However, if you accept and embrace THIS, then Authentic Action will arise in the world through You, for You will be a conduit for *our* unified loving Awareness to manifest in the physical world.

Why do I suggest that Awareness is loving? Because although when you dissolve in Awareness there is only THIS full vibrant everything and nothingness, once you ground the 'spiritual' in the 'physical' plane, Love is one of the two qualities of THIS which arises. Like the warmth felt from the radiating Sun, it is irrefutable. That sense of Love is seen to be the real meaning of Intelligence, now known to be alive in You. That's why Intelligent Love is one of the two inseparable qualities of Being. The other quality of Awareness is Peace of Mind. These two fundamental qualities of Being arise simultaneously, and are the very perfume of Life itself. Unmistakable and undeniable, they are the evidence of the transformation of consciousness. Peace of Mind and Intelligent Love are the subtle qualities of Awareness present before the arising of the primary thought of 'I AM'.

As the Beatle John Lennon said:

If someone thinks that Peace and Love are just a cliché that must have been left behind in the 60s, that's a problem. Peace and Love are eternal.

All versions, all appearances, all varieties are parts of THIS. The tree is THIS as a tree, the child THIS in the form of a child or the space in front of you THIS as thin air. To realise THIS, then stop thinking and really look. Look deeply at anything in nature, a tree, a flower, the sky – for when you leave the involuntary dialogue of the habitual mind long enough, you will naturally go beyond the boundaries of form. When you do – you will see and be THIS that YOU are.

Now Zen...

The koan is a treasure of Zen Buddhism. It is a brief paradoxical statement or question used to exhaust the intellect and the will, leaving the purged mind (or no-mind) open to an intuitive response. They include the well-known example, "What is the sound of one hand clapping?" When your mind gives up, gives in and surrenders to what is, the answer appears. One answer could be THIS.

In another example of a koan, the Monk Mayo is said to have asked: "What is Zen?" to which the Sixth Patriarch replied, "when your mind is not dwelling on the dualism of good and evil, what is your original face before you were born?" The question itself, in the words of Mr Spock is 'most illogical captain'. The answer is as well. Again, one possible answer could be THIS. The solution cannot be arrived at through a process of linear thought – but only by letting go of it. The answer is allowed to appear, rather than digging out or forcing an intellectual response. Surrendering allows you to see THIS. The answer to the koan cannot be found by delving into the memorised stockpiles of facts, figures and details. The intellect simply doesn't know. It cannot know. The answer lies beyond cerebral thought. All this points us towards an intuitive dimension of Universal Intelligence accessed beyond traditional conditioned responses. The question guides us towards the recognition that we *all* have an inner wisdom or knowingness which is present before thought, or "before you were born". THIS profound teaching doesn't negate or devalue thought – it simply puts thought in its place. *What-YOU-really-are* is ever-present Awareness. THIS is not reached through thought, but rather realised to be humankind's pure-minded reality once the individual lets go of the urge or need to think altogether.

So, it is impossible for you to reason THIS, to think THIS, to change THIS, to understand THIS, to attain THIS, to define THIS, to prove THIS or to control THIS. Letting go of everything you are not brings you to the awareness of *what-YOU-really-are*, which is THIS. Again, the YOU pointed to here is Being itself. It is yours and not yours, for it simply *IS* – here and now beyond individual identity.

THIS is within and encapsulating everything. You can't touch it because there is no separation, no gap and no duality. It's the indivisible One. It's all going on within the present unlimited-ness of itself. THIS is within you as you are within THIS. So is everyone and everything else. It is the ultimate Heart of *our* essence, and simply THIS.

7

∞ Surrender to THIS! ∞

In the physical dimension, people have a tendency to see surrender as giving up or losing, and it is often considered to be the epitome of failure. The sacred art of Surrender doesn't mean giving up, but facing, letting go and giving in – letting go of the mego's self-induced independence and giving in to the flow of Life. When we let go of our individual barriers, we find ourselves free to see and be the unbounded Universe.

The mego is conditioned to believe it is *the* pilot of *the* plane, but as THIS becomes more obvious, you discover the existence of the autopilot system. Then you take your hands off the joystick and really experience the joy of flying. THIS is flying without fear. It feels as if you have been swimming against the powerful current of 'bad' and 'difficult' experiences, struggling to get anywhere, when suddenly you realise that 'going with the flow' of the water is taking you to exactly where you need to be. Not always where you envisaged you'd like to be, but where you *need* to be to experience, learn and grow. Surrendering to the infinite THIS means consciously placing your life in the hands of Universal Intelligence, allowing your life to unfold in alignment with the Whole, for the betterment of the Whole (a Whole which of course always includes You). Not simply doing nothing and pretending there is no one with nothing to do, but living a life of contribution, integrity, value and purpose in this world as an Authentic Human Being. Then You will not only be helping yourself, but all 'others'.

The mego is 'seen through' in the process of Surrender. To Surrender to THIS means to stop fighting, a struggle the mego can't ever win because it's always trying to control realities and outcomes, fighting against the present moment which is *always* here and now, always THIS. You cannot change THIS; you just need the humility to accept it.

Letting go of the bossy addictive mind of the mego is a good thing. As the mego becomes increasingly aware of its impending transformation, it will panic, because it senses that it is being dragged to the 'edge of the cliff', which is a fearful, daunting prospect. Like a dictator being usurped, it will take desperate measures to hold on to power. And that's just it, for any entity bent on maintaining control is based in fear and not in Love. You cannot control THIS, but You can actively participate in its establishment within human consciousness and our world.

The ensuing panic of revolution causes the mego to look for ways out, to find escape routes. It does this by reopening deeply rooted patterns which still remain embedded in your consciousness. The brainwashing power of the mego is so cunning it will do anything it can to sustain the pretence that it, and it alone is the real you. To try and put off this revolt, the mego creates symptoms or dilemmas, such as loss of concentration or memory, headaches, fear, panic, tiredness, and just about any method of distraction or detour it can lay its hands on.

The most powerful tool the mego has is fear. It will recreate fearful scenarios in a multitude of ways, until you are ready to dive into the Universal SELF. It will take fear from the past and project it into the future to project a 'reason' why Surrender doesn't or cannot work:

It's all too simple; I mean do you really think I'm dumb enough to be taken in by THIS?

You want me to give in to THIS, a something I can't even see? Right...!

What will my friends and family say; people will think I've lost it...

But what will I do for a living and how will I pay my bills?

Next you'll be asking me to give everything I have to some religious cult...

I can't do this; I've got a partner / family and children…
What will people think of me?
How do I know I'll be alright? How can I trust THIS?
THIS is a scary and frightening idea, I don't like it.

You can see these are all fear-based projections. They are versions of self-identity which contain projections and associations with intelligence, being hoodwinked, trust and fear. And they are all methods of avoidance.

The way to overcome megoic fear is to face it head on. The greatest fear of the mego is its very own demise. So if you really want to see THIS, let go of your greatest fear, which for most people is the mego's belief in the finality of death. Death is inevitable in two dimensions of your being; the body and the mind of mego. But you are more than that, YOU are THIS. THIS was never born and can never die. The here and now is the evidence to THIS timeless, eternal Truth.

It seems like a lifetime ago now, but in my early forties, I received a 'mystical death experience' in which the fear of death was faced head on. I wanted to find the Truth with all my being, and so the opportunity presented itself. Needless to say, it wasn't how or what I expected.

To give you the abbreviated version, I fell to the floor and consciousness separated from the body. That is to say, 'I' was floating on the ceiling, and could clearly see the body was empty, appearing like a deserted shell washed up on the beach of life. In those first few moments, a brief panic took place, before fading away as I accepted the inevitability of what was taking place. I was no longer in control, or so it appeared. As I Surrendered to the idea of physical death, Life appeared in all its radiance and glory. I was overwhelmed by a powerful sense of Love and Peace, and for the first time in my life, I felt completely and utterly Whole and connected. I realised that the potent joy of being had always been 'here' alive in me. Always THIS. I realised

THIS to be the truth of my Soul. I realised THIS to be the Oneness of *all*. I realised THIS that YOU are.

So now it's your turn. Who do you choose to fly your plane, drive your car, and lead your life – which do you choose, fear or love?

The self-important authoritarian nature of the mego means it will always want to control what happens. Of course Life is something you cannot control, and many things take place beyond your control. When seemingly 'unfortunate' things take place, you cannot rely on the fear-based mego, for it will be in a state of panic and stress, only seeing life from its own centre. The mego sees a limited view of life, like looking through a pair of binoculars; it's a partial view of a much greater whole.

When you surrender to THIS, you enter an all-inclusive view, a wholistic impression of what is taking place, a naturally occurring stillness and balance allowing you to be calm and present. You will not only feel a deep sense of liberation by giving in to Life, but your life will flow better than ever, for you will be more accepting and no longer trying to change, manipulate or control outcomes. Surrendering to THIS isn't a problem because Life is inherently Love-ing and Peace-ful, so you will always be supported by Universal Intelligence. You may not realise you are an interconnected part of a greater Whole, but the Universe knows you are. You are loved by the Universe. YOU are inseparable from the Universe. Life will support you if you Surrender to its momentum and its expression. Surrendering to the Universe is a powerful Action which creates space for unrecognised potentials, for when the mego surrenders, it opens up a multiplicity of possibilities it would never have dreamt as being possible. The possibilities are unknown and beyond human imagination.

The deepest rewards in life will come when you surrender to THIS. That reward is the Reality of Life. It is not a material reward, but an eternal reward. Surrender to THIS is inevitable at some point, but in this moment it still requires your unconditional agreement to let go and dive into Universal Being. You must be ready to let go of the idea of self-importance and be open and available to the natural flow of Life itself. And if you do, you will be cared for and nourished in ways you cannot possibly imagine. If you're in doubt, just look up into the night sky sometime on a clear evening. If you feel a sense of wonder as you gaze at the miraculous architecture of the cosmos, and humbly appreciate just how miniscule a human being is in comparison to the whole, then maybe you're ready to realise the infinite YOU, the presence which permeates the totality.

The act of surrendering to THIS allows you to find *what-YOU-really-are* through an organic process of transformation or Change. That is Change with a capital C, because it is Authentic, and comes from the natural sharing momentum at the root of Being. Real Change comes from Love, and inspires yourself and others, for it is an expression of fulfilment from Spirit or Awareness itself.

So, surrendering your identity leads to Change via the transformation of your consciousness. It's not that you are finding something that nobody else has or is, it's simply you are courageous enough to find THIS which is here and now, present in us all and *what-YOU-really-are.*

And it doesn't end with Change. Out of non-reliance on the mego comes Action which is true, lasting and effective – synergetic Action from the Heart Stream of Consciousness. The act of Surrender allows the birthing of Change and Action.

When you truly Surrender, it is wholehearted and unconditional. These are pre-requisites. You trust the Universal Intelligence so completely that you put your life in its hands. And neither do you have mind-based projections of what will arise from your Surrender. Why not? Because your mind doesn't know, so it cannot answer the question. And who is it that wants a guarantee?

To really Surrender you must trust that Life brought you here for good reason, full of purpose and meaning. But don't imagine what Surrender will reveal, for to decide what is going to happen will mean that you create mental boundaries to the boundless. Trust that through the action of Surrender, Life will reveal not only *what-YOU-really-are*, but all You can be and do in the world. The conscious action of Surrender opens the door to Wholeness.

Approaching Surrender is the time when the seeker arrives at the edge of a cliff, and looks down, seeing how close one apparently is to one's own death. Fear arises. But if you are truly ready to Surrender, then something else takes over; the faith in Life itself, a 'spiritual' faith sensed at the core of your being. This gives rise to a radiant intuition which gives you the confidence and power to leap, and the ability to trust and let go. You will know when you're ready, but not from the head, for the act of Surrender is not rational in that sense. It is your consciousness which opens to the infinite sound of the Universe. When you're ready, you will take the leap.

You are approaching THIS when you recognise that viewing the ups and downs of life as a permanent personal battlefield really doesn't help you or anyone else. Life is not personal, it's Universal. The idea that life entirely centres on you simply creates further strain, stress and inevitable problems. When you recognise that un-surrendered action taken by the mego is in direct opposition to the Peace, Love and unity at the core of your being, you are getting ready. When you are fed up with the mego's projections of what is going to happen next, you are getting ready. The act of Surrender is the true meaning of a leap of faith. You've experienced enough separation in all its forms and recognise the mego as a fractionate state of being brought about by mind-made deliberations and dense emotional patterning. You are ready, willing and able to let go.

Arising from Surrender...

There are inevitable consequences arising from the act of Surrender. THIS is the act of the mego giving in to the Intelligence of Life, the individual merging in the Universal. THIS is the only act that simultaneously frees and connects you. You will never be the same again. Life will never be the same again.

From your rediscovery and reconnection with THIS Awareness, you open the doors of the mind to the limitless potential of Universal Action. Authentic Action isn't brought about by the wants or needs of individuated desire, for it is the natural expression of your living interconnectedness with the Whole. It comes from an alignment of inner and outer being. It is not deliberately designed to please everyone all the time, but it will come from an Authentic Whole-minded expression. To Act from Awareness isn't always soft and passive. Sometimes the most loving Action is to say 'no'. To Act from Awareness comes through not being attached to personal ideals and opinions, and allowing the transparent clear flow of the Heart Stream of Consciousness to be lived. It will not be a 'decision', but a following of our Nature.

When consciousness organically arises from THIS – then arising thought will be led by Universal Awareness, and not overlooked or untapped as it was with the mego. Then we Act from, for and with the Whole in mind.

So we can say that Surrender leads to the outpouring of Change and Action. Or in other words reconnecting with the Oneness of Life transforms your consciousness, and empowers you to Act in ways that express and share Intelligent Love. It doesn't mean that you'll be a saint, or not be a saint, but it does mean that you will be able to realise the Universal Truth of *what-YOU-really-are*, which is the catalyst to being You and all You can share with the world.

Authentic Change and Action take place as THIS is stabilised, integrated and grounded in consciousness. When the individual mind has inverted on itself, and there are no further obstructions in consciousness, then Awareness seemingly appears. THIS appears. I write 'seemingly' because THIS was/is here all the time and you never even knew it. THIS, seen as the present moment, is the founding unified being-ness of All, an infinite Truth which we and the vast bulk of humankind somehow overlooked. THIS is the key to world peace, and the actuality of a better world for *all* life forms. So THIS is not only the now, but *what-YOU-really-are*. More than that, it's what everybody else is too. And there's more… for THIS is the ever-present all-permeating pure energy Consciousness which naturally emanates Love via the Heart Stream of Consciousness. A constant flow you can sense, know and consciously Act from, for, and with.

8

∞ The Non-duality of THIS & More ∞

THIS is the knowingness that the mysterious YOU, SELF, Awareness, Consciousness, Being, are One and the same. Non-duality is the dimension of no-other, of everything and no-thing.

So here we are. THIS moment is the doorway to seeing THIS. But THIS is anonymous and Universal, as you have to let go of individual identity to directly experience non-personal Awareness.

You are Awareness. You are Consciousness. You are Presence. You are Being.

All of the above are *what-YOU-really-are*.

In the depths of the Non-dual experience, any and all sense of 'I' dissolves. You discover that there is no 'I' in Awareness. And as I explained earlier, the true Non-dual experience is marked by absolute stillness of mind, pure Mind or no-mind – you pick the description you prefer. THIS is the inexplicable mystery, for there are no words or thoughts taking place in pure Awareness, not even the arising of 'I AM'. The physical senses have been transcended along with the urge, desire or need to think as no 'other' or 'else' is seen to exist.

It is only as the dual function of the mind moves us out of Non-duality that we get a sense of what THIS is. It is only when we come out of the vibrant mysterious stillness that we recognise THIS. That's why I pointed to the subtle sensing of the primary qualities of Awareness as being Intelligent Love and Peace of Mind, followed by the arising of the primary thought 'I AM'. So in truth, the overflowing silence and vibrant stillness of Awareness is the sole Authentic Non-dual experience. 'I AM' which arises out of THIS, is the One-dual expression of our most profound sense of being, and the primary thought arising in the mind. THIS underlies and permeates each and every movement of the mind, even the primary thought 'I AM'.

I mentioned THIS in my previous book, Naked Being:

There is nothing outside of THIS, for it is the silent awakening of the present moment, the complete conscious recognition of the now. When presently aware of the pure Consciousness YOU are, then THIS is the clearest description of that fundamental Reality.

Paradoxically this means that when you Surrender to Awareness, there is no one left to identify with. The absolute sense of 'me' really does 'go'. There is just THIS. Nobody can truthfully say 'I have realised the SELF' for when YOU are Awareness, there is no 'I' present to make the realisation. In the Non-duality of Awareness, subject and object merge as One. There is no need to distinguish or identify. No commentary and no comment. In Awareness, the capacity to engage the cog-like mechanism of the mind is disengaged. The mind is still there, but it is inactive, pure and unmodified. It is only on returning to the activity of the mind that recognition and understanding of THIS actually takes place.

Non-duality is often understood as being something intellectual and a difficult principle to grasp or understand. But when you see THIS is not an understanding, but the founding experience of Life available in *each and every* moment, there's no reason for you to wait for the right time – in fact, realising THIS will only ever happen here and now!

In many ways Non-duality is easy to see, because it is always here. You are never separate from THIS. The problem the mind has with Non-duality is that it is so simple to grasp, it's often overlooked. It's not such a big thing. You do not need to be a genius or 'special' to know THIS; you just need to Surrender the mind to its Universal root. Each moment is an ever-open window to the ocean of Awareness.

SELF-Realisation & Enlightenment

Glimpsing THIS is not the same as SELF-Realisation. SELF-Realisation is a permanent and continuous experience of the SELF as a non-identity. To live life as Awareness itself. To be YOU, to be the non-identity of Spirit. Spirit needs neither body nor mind to be, and yet at this point in the human evolution of consciousness, we are moving towards the acceptance and integration of the Body-Mind-Spirit being we presently are. For you have a body, you have a mind, and yet YOU are Divine Spirit.

A glimpse of the SELF leads to 'other' glimpses, and to Soul-realisation, whereas *complete and permanent* dissolution in Awareness as Awareness is the mark of a SELF-Realised being. It's a bit like finding an infinite ocean of Oneness, and having the opportunity to dip your toes in before returning home (the glimpse) or have one foot in the ocean and one grounded on land (the multidimensional Soul) or the timeless permanence of being the Ocean (the SELF).

SELF-Realisation is *very* rare. For billions of people there is no leap from mego to a permanent and lasting non-identity as Awareness, but there are many who will infer this, or want to believe that it is so for them. As you can see from the example of the ocean of Oneness above, an experience of Awareness does not necessarily mean complete and permanent immersion in the SELF. For the Unividual, the experience of Awareness is an inter-mediate stage, and a window to the realisation of the Soul. However, a growing number of people around the world are having glimpses and Oneness and Universality are slowly but surely affecting humankind. The worldview consciousness is shifting, and it is doing so as increasing numbers share their consistent experiences of the Universal.

To be Authentically SELF-Realised, consciousness must be absolutely free of any and all obstructions, or *vasanas* (subtle psycho-emotional patterns arising in the mind). The direct experience of pure Consciousness then can be permanently and continuously known, as it is matched by the pure Mind of the seeker. Only then can it be abiding and ever-present.

When you 'think' you've overcome these vasanas or individual patterning, then you have not. The only proof of their dissolution is not found in thought, but in the absence of them arising. Initially, it is obvious when you are opinionated, angry, moody, obstinate, and resentful as we learn to recognise and accept the fallibility of our individuality. Through a transparent listening and watching they become less addictive and infrequent as they are gradually recognised and cleared. It may take a week, a month, a year or a decade before the next vasana arises, and they do so in increasingly subtle forms, sometimes catching you by complete surprise. It is the permanent and lasting purging of the individual mind together with the direct experience of unmodified Consciousness which leads to the Divine Reality of SELF-Realisation.

However, the next stage in the evolution of human consciousness does not concern the mind's ideal of a world in which everyone is SELF-Realised, but rather the actualisation of Soul consciousness (Soulness) here on Earth. From the convergence of inner and outer being, a marriage takes place between the Human and the Spirit. Once this occurs, You find yourself standing at the water's edge, with one foot in the ocean and one foot on land, as the Universal Intelligence of Life unfolds naturally, without hindrance or obstruction. You are perfect and imperfect, empty and full. You are open and available to live the consciousness of a Universal Human Being or Unividual.

There are growing numbers of people who have glimpsed the SELF, but who interpret THIS as something final and completed. They think they are SELF-Realised or have reached the mind's finality of being 'Awakened'. If you are sat in a room with a genuinely SELF-Realised being, there will be a tangible energy of Peace of Mind and Intelligent Love, because these are the inseparable and fundamental qualities of Being-Consciousness-Bliss. Someone who is SELF-Realised will emanate and radiate these qualities in all dimensions of their being because their consciousness and Consciousness itself are unified, or as close as it can be to THIS. Not only that, but they will exemplify THIS at all times in all places effortlessly. These rare few are as close as human consciousness can come to Spirit in the flesh. They are signposts to the future evolution of human consciousness, but not the next 'step', for You are the next step.

What we're moving towards here is how THIS enters the world as You. Of course, THIS is already and always here, but only You can be an outlet for THIS. To copy another is fruitless and empty. Being You as only You can be is the Authentic gift and contribution only You can share.

You must find your own way. Unless you find it yourself, it will not be your own way and will take you nowhere.
– Sri Nisargadatta

THIS is how a human is able to feel, sense and express their invaluable, deepest and fullest sense of Spirit or Being in the world. You hold the secret to a miraculous yet ordinary contribution, a Universal contribution which is unique to You, yet beneficial for the Whole. It is integral and unique, the living paradox of a Whole-part.

The seeing or recognition of the Universal may bring about the end of seeking, but it is not the end of THIS. There is no beginning and no end to THIS ever-present, ever-growing and ever-expanding human consciousness. Even the Universe itself is expanding as these words are being written. For the vast majority of the world's population, the knowing that YOU are Awareness is a stepping stone to the next paradigm in human consciousness. The seeing of *what-YOU-really-are* is the catalyst allowing Awareness to appear in the world as You. We will explore this further in part two.

And what of enlightenment – how does this fit in to the equation? Well, any person who tells you they are enlightened – has not transcended the thought that they are enlightened – and so has not truly let go. For why would any announcement be made or confirmation be sought? Who would seek it? And why would the idea arise in one who is truly free of the labels of the conceptual mind? If they were truly free, there would be no need of comparison and nothing to let go *or* to hold on to. There would be neither enlightenment nor ignorance.

The thought, 'I am enlightened', or the question, 'Am I enlightened?', arise in a time-based mind seeking to be identified with enlightenment. The question itself is posed by a separate mind which thinks it is not enlightened. On the other hand, anyone who believes they are *not* enlightened – has not let go of the thought that they are not. The grasping individual mind seeks to define, label and confine. Enlightenment is not a question of is she or isn't he, but the permanent and continuous realisation of the enlightened Awareness of *our* Being; like asking the question 'Am I the SELF?' – when the idea of 'Am I enlightened?' no longer arises, then it is outgrown and no longer sought or needed. Living the Authentic example of all You are is the way and the truth. The art of living in Wholeness is to be fully and transparently You, for then life will take place in harmony with the Heart Stream of Consciousness, and THIS will feed and nurture the Whole.

It is kind of funny that many seeking the idea of enlightenment do so in order to liberate themselves. They seek a place or time when 'they' will be free and 'they' will not suffer, or 'they' will know – all of which appear to be selfish beliefs of the mego seeking that which it thinks it lacks.

The commercialised Non-dual view on the dissolution of the individual is an incomplete sharing. The idea that when you glimpse or recognise Awareness there is no longer a 'person' that can suffer because the mego has been 'eliminated' – is a partial or intermediate understanding. To seek the end of personal suffering by clinging to the non-identity of formlessness is the continuation of another form of illusion and avoidance, and one which will require further attention in time owing to the subtleties of the vasanas. You will always get what you need to grow, but you may not always be conscious of THIS.

In the silent vibrant Awareness which transcends speech and thought, there is no one, and of course no suffering. If we view all forms of Life, including the duality of falling in love with another as equally unreal, then this remains true. However, if we engage fully with all dimensions and layers of our Animal-Spirit being, then the Wholeness of Life is realised to be all-inclusive and non-negating. THIS is present and integrated in all dimensions. What THIS means is non-suffering belongs to no one rather than some-one who has realised the SELF. Are you really no one with no thoughts and nothing to do, nothing to contribute to life? It's just as easy for the mind to non-identify with your formless Nature as it is to mistakenly identify with the idea of a completely separate form.

When we are grounded and engaged in awakening to the presence of the Soul, suffering arises, but it is not owned. Like the mego, you do not have to go along with the idea. It's not that it doesn't arise at all, for this would be a claim with the distinct 'whiff' of avoidance. That would be like saying, 'No, no… it never rains in England' which would be the mind clinging to denial and preference. And likewise, if thoughts of love, compassion, helping and sharing arise – in THIS moment do they arise to no-one, some-one or every-one? You tell me.

You are not seeking THIS in order to become a non-person, but to be a Whole person. It is not about escape but integration. You simply need to empty your mind to see THIS. The disappearance of the mego doesn't necessitate the death of mind and personality. Consciousness is multidimensional, so when you are ripened by the living recognition of Awareness, the Unividual persona emerges.

In time you even let go of what THIS is. As the sixth-century and Third Chinese Patriarch Seng-Ts'an writes in *Verses on the Faith-Mind*:

Although all dualities arise from the One, do not be attached even to ideas of this One.

As the flower of Awareness unfolds from the One, it is seen to be present in all parts and a Whole. When you are ready, the holding on to formlessness drops away like a ripe fruit, for individual consciousness is naturally filled with the Universal Wholeness of Life. Only now do you embody Awareness, and share THIS with the world. THIS reveals both the voice and song of the Soul. You will say, do and be the Universal THIS in your own unique way. THIS is the integration of left and right brain, the coming together of the head and heart and the blossoming evolutionary human consciousness of One-duality.

So, what does a Unividual awakening to the consciousness of their Soul look like? How do they act? Someone who knows and lives THIS may appear as anyone at any time. They do not have to be Saints, Gurus or Teachers – and they wouldn't *necessarily* need to be sat in silent meditation under a tree 'Aum-ing' for days on end. But then again, they might. After all, they are all simply versions of *what-YOU-really-are*. They are not confined or confineable, for they are free in the knowingness that why they are here is propelled by a choice-less Surrender to the Heart-stream of Consciousness. They are free from identifying with the idea of any role they should or shouldn't play. They are free and open to the flow and manifestation of Universal Action. Inevitably, they would never wander far away from the empow-ering yet humble knowledge that Life is One, and the living Reality of Divine presence. They would be givers more than takers. They could be and are anyone, introvert and extrovert, for it is not about a specific personality or role. They would still have character and individuation. They are not Zombies. They would still be human beings, warts and all, but with an unshakeable Universal outlook. They could be as soft as a flower or as loud as thunder, or both. They would transcend any idea of perfection, or what you imagine perfection to be. They would be Authentic. They would uniquely and intuitively follow the Heart Stream of Consciousness. They would live in the knowledge and presence of God-Brahman. In other words, they would be just like YOU and share THIS without labelling or judgement.

So where is THIS taking us?

If we continue the same practice we started, then we continue letting go. If we continue letting go, we will not only let go of the mego, but of residual identification with formlessness too. You come full circle. You have been to the top of the mountain of Awareness, realised the One indivisible Spirit SELF of Brahman, and come back down the other side. Without following an accepted or specified route, seeking ends, but as it does, the expression of Awareness in the world through You (awakening to the presence of the Soul) begins.

As the ninth century Ch'an Buddhist Master Qingyuan Weixin noted, there are three notable stages of awakening in the human journey. The first stage is seeing the mountain as a mountain and water as water (conventional duality); the second stage is seeing the mountain not as a mountain and water not as water (the Non-duality of the Absolute); and the third stage, seeing the mountain as the mountain and water as water (the One-duality of the Whole-part). Only in stage three does consciousness integrate the conventional and the Absolute.

Living THIS awakening, perhaps what You now 'do' in life is what you imagined, perhaps not, but it will always be exactly what is needed for You and the Whole. You will know, and get on with it, whatever it is. You will Act from Change, and Change from Action.

In awakening to the presence of your Soul, your role becomes one of sharing and expressing the Universal in the actuality of the world. The Soul acknowledges the One both in and as an infinite number of expressions and appearances. If THIS impulse draws me to make chairs, then I make Chairs. If it means I sing, then I Sing. Whatever one does carries an undeniable Authentic quality unique to You. The 'I' that is the 'doer' is not separate, but recognised as a Unividual expression of the One.. It is duality lived in conscious symbiosis with the One, the Non-dual integrated with the dual, and in this sense we may call it One-duality.

In One-duality we realise the all-encompassing presence of Non-dual Awareness – but from within THIS loving core there emerges an active wholistic 'wordly' consciousness. A sacred sense of duality arises, one which is inexplicably linked to the earthly manifestation of our Non-dual Essence.

The idea that the body, mind and persona are illusory is left behind through the acceptance and integration of consciousness in all dimensions of being, for by grounding and establishing Awareness in the wholistic mind of the human, Wholeness appears. THIS is consciousness awakening to the dimension of the Soul, the 'reborn' persona converged with, yet emerging from the Non-dual Reality. The ray of sunshine aware of its integral relationship with Source. It is a natural blossoming of an Authentic multidimensional being whose consciousness in essence is inseparable from the Universal. Through the dimension of awakening to the Soul, THIS is shared in human consciousness via One-duality.

When we see from identification with form, then the formless does not exist.

When we see from non-identification with formlessness, then all form is illusory.

When we see both, then the Whole of what and who we are is

grounded in the One all-inclusive multidimensional consciousness.

Now there is an Authentic 'me' with the underlying experience and knowledge of the 'not-me'. They are lived as one without preference or discrimination. There is a no separation, for they are fused together and simultaneously true. THIS appears by accepting all dimensions of what constitutes a human being. You are Spirit (formlessness) in the form of an Animal. You might prefer to think 'highly intelligent animal thank you!' – but take a long, good hard look at the world we live in, and you will find that this is a dubious presumption.

We have divorced ourselves from the essential Love and Peace at *our* core and gone about life as if it were some sort of smash and grab raid, getting the most we can. We have pillaged the natural abundance of the planet, without a care in the world, just so we can 'prove' ourselves by having more than the next person. We have believed we are what we own, that ownership is the way to fulfilment. How wrong we were. We have been taken in by the idea that physical appearance is the most important aspect of who we are, when it is the least. We have believed that our thoughts are who we are. We have even believed we are nothing but an empty lifeless dream.

But we all have the opportunity to Change. We have the opportunity to Act. Authentic Changes and Actions emerge from the Heart of Being, and contain the 'spiritual' power to transform consciousness. You are a channel of Awareness, a conduit through which Love and Peace can be revealed in the world. So, from the indifference of Oneness, you become inspired to make a difference. Yes, make a difference, not because the Action or Actions make you feel and appear more important than another, but because it is *our* Nature, *our* Being calling You to do so, calling You to Act for the Whole, and to implement that Action wholeheartedly in the world for the benefit of all.

That's not to say you must do THIS alone. You must just do what is true to You, for when aligned with the Heart Stream of

Consciousness, You will be sharing pure Consciousness through the window of the Unividual mind, and, at this point in human evolution there is no greater contribution You can make.

So, don't copy an idea of what you should be. Just BE yourself fully. Don't overlook or ignore what arises in *your* consciousness. Then you will uncover THIS inexplicable silent and vibrant mystery. THIS is the window to meaning, purpose, expression and fulfilment. What you've been seeking all the time *was* the Authentic You. You in all dimensions, a Whole yet dynamic You awakening in the world with a pathway unfolding in every direction in every moment.

Now you're really ready to be You.

And I thank You for THIS.

My Soul bows to your Soul.

Part Two

Who

9

∞ Escaping the Non-duality Trap ∞

Let's recap a little before we move on, to be sure everything is clear. The initial step we took was through the window of THIS present moment, into the non-personal dimension of pure Awareness. So we went through the eternal window of THIS to uncover *what-YOU-really-are*. Now, THIS is a place many people get lost.

Spiritual bypass, work and philosophy

In the West's contemporary presentation of Non-duality or what is referred to as Neo-Advaita, you are being sold nothing by no one. It has to be that way in Neo-Advaita because it is a philosophy based on nihilism and negation wherein the world, the teacher, and you the individual are all considered to be unreal. Sitting there, watching and listening to another (!), you are getting an impression of the Awareness we *all* are. But the truth is you don't need to go anywhere or pay anything for that privilege, just be still, listen, and look inside yourself for THIS will always be here. It can't be bought from another, for you will never find YOU by going somewhere, but rather being nowhere. The idea of the mego becoming the non-identity of Awareness and never suffering again is a great sales pitch, and another partial truth at best.

People can experience profound suffering by being disconnected from who and what they are, so the idea of discovering an immediate end to suffering is widely appealing. The belief in a 'fast-food' style instant awakening, and clinging to the idea that 'There is nothing to do and no one to be' when there is still a need to face individual patterning, is a sign of continued avoidance. If you approach Non-duality as a miraculous cure without being prepared to do your own work, then sadly you are only fooling yourself.

When you have not faced up to the necessary work of clearing the dense, negative patterning within the mind, it's easy to be attracted to the proposition of an immediate 'fix'. To consider an understanding or the glimpse alone as being final and complete, and to believe that you have reached the ultimate awakened state from the experience, is another form of avoidance or what is typically known as *spiritual bypass*. Spiritual bypass refers to the mind's tendency to create a fake version of Awareness or Spirit in an attempt to prematurely secure it as your absolute identity. Some practices and teachings make this an inevitable trap. As a consequence, should it happen to you, at some point you will undergo a relapse in consciousness. The only solution is to return to the patterning which caused your 'fall from grace', to face it, let it go and live THIS. Spiritual bypass is a defence mechanism which takes place because of our desire to avoid facing up to the everyday realities of living in the world. Below, I have drawn a list of examples and causes to give you an idea of what spiritual bypass can involve, and what to look out for:

1. An avoidance or denial of our own imperfections or negative patterning.
2. A subtle but inflated sense of one's spiritual attainments.
3. Overly concerned in how one appears to be, think and act rather than living a balanced and wholesome Authenticity.
4. A pink and fluffy view of life, accompanied by the denial of painful personal, societal and global realities.
5. It can happen as a reaction to a painful personal shock (e.g the death of a loved one).
6. The likelihood of inconsistent, variable and ungrounded states of consciousness.
7. The belief that you were (in a past life) or are an

important key, or are 'awakened' and enlightened when not.

8. A hankering for, or identification with, paranormal and supernatural phenomena. A deluded view of one's spiritual abilities.

9. Overly nice to the point of being superficial.

10. Lacking Divine humility.

Whether you like it or not, if you want to really know *what-YOU-really-are*, you must untangle your psycho-emotional patterning to the point where the mind is inverted on itself and nothing arises in consciousness. Only you can do THIS. The consciousness of the individual then dives into the fundamental pure Consciousness it emerges from. Do not be fooled into the idea that there is no work involved. You must do the preparatory groundwork first. You can't simply pay a fee, book a time and get awakened. If you believe that, you'll find you'll keep going back until you've convinced yourself in some hollow way that it's true. In the end, what it takes is for you to realise that the only way THIS is going to work is through you. Nobody else can do THIS for you.

That is not to suggest that group or solo practices are fruitless or pointless. Authentic practices regularly undertaken can be a great help. But it is worth considering the possibility that they provide the most momentum to our journey when we do not allow the practice or tool to become an addiction, for if that is the case, then the mind is delaying what is essentially a natural and intuitive process of introspection and self-knowledge. Authentic Teachers who share THIS can be a great help for a while. And yet any Authentic Teacher is simply pointing to what YOU already and always are. If, as is often the case, it takes time for the seeker to see and ground THIS in their consciousness, then hopefully the commercial rewards for the Teacher do not outweigh the spiritual intention. Use your head *and* follow your heart, for

THIS is beyond both.

While it is true from the Non-dual silence of Awareness that there is nobody there and nothing to do, there is more to THIS. The idea of 'nothing to do' *can* be a route to avoidance. The still, silent Reality of nothing and everything is Awareness. So, to rest in the mind's understanding of Awareness without exemplifying THIS in the world, suggests you are caught in the Non-dual trap. If you were truly absorbed in Non-duality, there would be no thought, no idea, no question, and no expression, just THIS. All would be the mysterious and indefinable 'God experience' of Sat-cit-ānanda or *Being-Consciousness-Bliss* in which the empty stillness YOU are would be brimming with life and entirely full. (The Sanskrit expression Sat-cit-ānanda is the subjective experience of God or Brahman, an expression which represents the same meaning as the Intelligent Love and Peace, the primary qualities of Being as described earlier in the book).

So, in order to express and embody THIS, the mental and physical dimensions of duality are engaged. If you are caught in the *idea* of Non-duality, you are simply clinging to an intellectual understanding. Then you begin to think or believe that you're 'awakened' when THIS is not a thought. You cannot 'think' yourself into Awareness. Awareness is known via the cessation of thought. All you need do is still the mind to see THIS is true.

So, the glimpsing of Awareness remains incomplete when you have not done the personal work of clearing your individual patterning, or that you lack the knowledge and meaning of the Awareness experience. We will look at the meaning of knowledge and experience shortly when we discuss the various states or levels of samadhi. The combination of the knowledge and the experience together is what allows THIS to be understood and grounded in human consciousness. The experience and the knowledge together *is* the work, for it is the combination of the direct experience and the knowledge of what THIS is which allows it to be integrated into the consciousness of the human being.

In the *philosophy* of Advaita, the SELF is the only Reality, it is Reality, and we are *all* already the SELF. But the *practicality* of Advaita is that there is work to be done before the truth of THIS can be grounded and lived on a daily basis. Doing the work means initially coming to the point where the thought 'I am not the SELF' no longer arises. We are enlightened Awareness, but is THIS stabilised and interwoven in your consciousness? Is THIS presence truly sensed? Is THIS integrated in your being? Or have you got work to do? Radical honesty is a powerful tool and a requirement for THIS. In time, even 'I am the SELF' will have no requirement to arise in consciousness, as You actually begin to live THIS in the world through awakening to the presence of your Soul. Then You are realised to be simultaneously integral and unique, a Whole-part. In THIS there is value, peace and fulfilment.

To the mind of mego, the opportunity to purchase freedom is a very attractive proposition. The mego might think *'Just think what I can do with all that freedom!'* – because the mego is very happy looking at some separate 'other' telling them they've got something 'else' missing. That's how the dualistic mind of the materialistic mego thinks and works. It'll even pay for the privilege, in a half-hearted attempt to buy freedom and delay it at the same time. That's because by having a ticket, it avoids having to do the work, a work which inevitably leads to its own downfall. Subtle and sly is our friend the mego.

So, by all means follow the fast-food style immediate awakening, but for a lasting and balanced transformation of consciousness, experience and knowledge need to come hand in hand. You must do your own work to realise Awareness. If you copy another or avoid the preparatory work, it will doubtless return to kick you in the backside at some point later on, perhaps in a more obvious form, until you finally face what you need to face in order for THIS to be apparent. You can't grow a rose if you don't prepare the earth properly, or, in time, its beauty will be strangled by the weeds.

While it is true that everything is One, it is also true that THIS is present and alive in *ALL-that-we-are* and all that *IS*. To live the Truth of grounding, stabilising and living THIS, to be THIS in all dimensions of our Body-Mind-Spirit being, we emerge 'reborn' from the Non-dual non-identity. That letting go of Non-dual Awareness isn't an effort or a choice, for it takes place when you are ripe, and it is as natural as the fledgling leaving the nest. When it happens, you will know. When it happens, you will understand. When you begin to merge with the presence of the Soul, you will know it to be True, for the question of 'Who am I?' and 'What am I?' are not only answered but alive in You and the world. Now there is the converged presence of Universal Awareness, Individuality *and* thought, but no doubting their existence and unified reality.

Who is what?

Until this point in the book, Awareness has been described as *what-YOU-really-are* and not who You are. This is because Awareness can only ever be *what-YOU-really-are*, for it is 'I-less' and anonymous. It has no identity. There is no one who is Awareness, for Awareness simply *IS*. Although YOU are Awareness, it is a YOU which is not claimable for yourself, for it is an acceptance of the Divine Reality. Awareness is not 'mine' or 'yours' but simply THIS. It is the realisation that the trunk or body of the tree is inseparable from the branches and the leaves. For the branches and leaves are as real as the body of the tree itself. All is THIS.

The wholistic truth of *who* you are comes through awakening to the consciousness of You, the Soul. For the purpose of this explanation, depending on 'where' you are or are not, here are three simplified versions of identity and non-identity:

1. The mego is a partial and fractionate identity which is the dormant or partially conscious soul confining itself to the world of form (the mego). Individual – *duality*- **self, you.**
2. Awareness is the persona free non-identity (pure energy Consciousness). Universal – *Non-duality* – **SELF, YOU.**
3. The Soul is the mediator between duality and Non-duality, the hybrid conscious bridge between the Individual and the Universal partnership. Aware of universal and self-identity, it is the consciousness which naturally propels us into Action in the world. Unividual – *One-duality* – **Self, You.**

Again, we will look at this in further detail in the following chapters.

The Non-dual experience allows us to realise the coreless core we *all* share. Awareness is the Ground of Being from which we awaken to the living presence of the Soul. A mind identified with separation is the mego. A no-mind not-identified with non-separation is the non-mego. A consciousness freed from identifying with mind and no-mind, separation and non-separation means that You are awakening to Soulness, free of higher and lower, ego and non-ego, seeking and not-seeking. Although it is free from the idea of the finality of being 'awakened', there is the living realisation that it is alive, blossoming like a flower, and in this sense, awakening in consciousness and the world.

If we continue to cling to the idea of Non-duality then words and attitudes can become quite at odds to the forethought qualities of Love and Peace which emanate from and through Awareness. The constant negation of everything as 'not-real' is an abbreviationof the Whole. Acceptance of the Divine totality and an abiding awareness of the non-separation between form and formlessness allows the presence of the Soul to stabilise in consciousness. THIS reveals that the Soul is not an illusion as philosophised by some forms of Advaita.

The SELF is everyone's essential Nature; it is what all IS, *what* YOU are - but not *who* You are. When the SELF appears as the foreground of consciousness, there is no 'I' available to claim it. It is Divine Awareness, not yours or mine, but ours and more. It doesn't belong to anybody and is not a form of identity. It is the One True SELF, and cannot be claimed or fully explained. It is Brahman, the Divine mystery in which you exist but cannot be found. So the Whole is realised through the direct experience of the SELF. It is from the established grounding or integration of THIS experience that a human being becomes wholistically conscious of the inseparable parts of the One Whole. The consciousness of the Unividual Soul appears as the living paradox that You are both integral and unique. THIS is the One-dual realisation that You are a Whole-part. You exist within Brahman-God-Awareness, and Brahman-God-Awareness exists within You.

When the mego has been let go, there is a tendency to believe that addiction in all its varied guises is also gone for good. However, because the truth of the Non-dual glimpse is the still, silent dissolution in Awareness, it may be sought once the duality of the mind is active again. It is just as easy for someone to be addicted to the idea of formlessness as it is for them to be hypnotised by the commentary of the mego.

When you glimpse THIS, the mind doesn't dissolve. The mind continues. What takes place from glimpsing Awareness is an expansion of space and transparency within your consciousness. Thoughts arise, and you see them for what they are. The thoughts the mego believed as being the real you are exposed as fraudulent and untrue. You no longer blindly follow the mind's thoughts, because you have experienced the blissful pure Mind of Awareness without the presence of any thoughts whatsoever. It is like you have caught a thief trying to rob you of your Divine birthright and inheritance. The more you do not engage and follow conditioned thoughts, the more they are exposed, and the greater the space.

The greater the space, the more grounded and stabilised pure-minded Awareness becomes in your consciousness.

YOU are Awareness. You know THIS from both the understanding and the experience. One without the other doesn't work. If you come to THIS from one side only, you will either be left with a purely intellectual understanding or an experience you cannot fully comprehend. Whatever happens, it takes time for the dissolution of the mego to stabilise and for THIS to be grounded in your consciousness. You will only find and live the Authenticity of your Soul by facing and letting go of each and every discovery, including *what-YOU-really-are*. Let go of everything, including the idea of letting go, and live what remains.

The present commercialisation of spirituality is a direct reflection of our society. We not only want it, but we want it right now, immediately. The mind that wants it now is not the mind that consciously lives THIS. It's another mego trip. You can't have what you stand in the way of unless you don't stand in the way of THIS.

Nowadays spiritual fads are rapidly increasing. The latest this, the best that. People want to have and to own the latest versions of whatever in order to feel value and worth. THIS is nothing new. It has no cost. It's not on display, but always here. No one person has it, and yet we all may realise it if we are prepared to look hard enough.

The real work to undertake is to uncover that which creates blocks in the natural flow of consciousness, for it is these addictive tendencies which prevent recognition of our pure-minded Awareness. It is these obstacles of the psyche which obstruct the Peace and Love residing at, and flowing from, our core. THIS is not complicated and everyone can find it through stilling the mind using introspective practices such as meditation. When you still the mind, you begin to really listen and see. Awareness is pure Mind. What is it that prevents your mind from being still? When you are annoyed what is at the root of your annoyance? It is never anyone 'else'. Whatever gets in your way is also the remedy if you dig deep enough. Take a look at the breathing exercises at the end of the book, as they may help you in THIS work.

Twenty-first-century Non-duality for the masses offers a 'fantastic deal' with the latest special offer being the instant finality of being awakened. However, any sense of the future role of individuality is frequently negated, and the explanations of THIS are void of any of the wider understandings of flow, integration or ripening. The common repeated approach to human ethics "There is no right or wrong" is a partial under-standing, and shows the person presenting this concept has yet to develop a more integral consciousness. The point of reaching the depths of Awareness is to move consciousness towards the living presence of the Soul.

The mego believes it is separate from awakening, when in reality it is THIS in every moment. Likewise, there are many 'reasons' why we may get 'stuck' in the 'idea' of Non-duality. They mostly come from a misunderstanding of what THIS is. People start to believe they are 'awakened', when they have just grasped the idea or thought of THIS. So there can be an 'assumption' that they have reached the end, and as they cling to that idea, they deny the direct experience of THIS.

The assumption that the ups and downs of life are completely over, or that there is nothing left to do and no one to do it, is a quagmire which denies people the right to live the universal potential of their sacredness. In short, there is no Heart and Soul in such a teaching. It lacks Love. If it lacks Love, then it is not THIS.

Samadhi & Science

As we know, it is clearly possible to cling to an idea, rather than be fully conscious of something. Clinging is not the Reality, but a faculty of the mind. The freedom of THIS lies within, beyond or behind thought. Effectively, THIS is directly experienced through a still-minded 'meditational' state referred to as samadhi. You do not see THIS through listening or accepting another version, but through direct experience.

The root of the Hindu word samadhi means to 'bring together'. It is the mind focussed on an empty yet full single point of absorption, the mind focussed on THIS. In the 'deepest' samadhi, dissolution of the individual is so complete that all sense of 'self' disappears, and subject and object are completely absorbed into each other. There are many types or layers of samadhi. According to David Godman in his book *Be As You Are – The teachings of Ramana Maharshi* p.156:

The following brief definitions formulated by Sri Ramana should be sufficient to guide the uninitiated through the terminological jungle of samadhi:

1. *Holding on to reality is samadhi.*
2. *Holding on to reality with effort is savikalpa samadhi.*
3. *Merging in reality and remaining unaware of the world is nirvikalpa samadhi.*
4. *Merging in ignorance and remaining unaware of the world is sleep.*
5. *Remaining in the primal, pure, natural state without effort is sahaja nirvikalpa samadhi.*

What I am trying to show here is that there are various states or plateaus of realisation as we uncover and integrate the Reality of pure Awareness. It is possible to 'experience' Awareness with partial or constant effort. That requires a subject and an object. Experiences of Awareness arise from the conscious presence and use of duality.

The Non-dual truth of Awareness is a silent negation of *all* differences. There is no difference between the realiser of the

SELF, and the world or universe. This is because pure Awareness is indivisible, and yet, in the physical plane or dimension of human experience, there is the appearance, play and reaction through the division of matter. The consciousness of the Soul sees itself as a Whole-part, and experiences the joy and freedom of THIS.

The Earth is rotating at 1000 mph. This is a true scientific measurement relative to our environment and yet is it your experience? Are you aware that at this very moment you are revolving like a spinning top at over 1000 mph? The Earth travels around the Sun at 66,666 mph – are you aware of that? Does it matter? Again, what is true to the human being is only relative to our dimension of experience and/or understanding. There are infinite expressions of the One, with the One present within, behind and beyond any single thing. None of them lack THIS, for THIS is presence itself, within everything and no-thing. And yet, the physical dimension is living proof of THIS as a denser expression of itself as form. Form and formlessness are insepa-rable yet essential as the expression of Life and the Universe. A Non-duality which denies the Soul disempowers the Love flowing in You and through You. THIS that is no-thing is the living presence of everything. THIS in itself doesn't negate the existence of the multiplicity of form, for that would be reinstating a sense of separation between THIS which has form and THIS which is formless. Body and mind are not illusory, simply denser 'forms' of THIS which gives rise to, and which permeates *all* forms. THIS is both core and substance of all that IS. There is nowhere THIS is not. It is in me, as it is in you, us and the world, the Universe, but only recognised from stripping back to the essence of the mind, and revealing pure Consciousness. It is THIS knowingness which allows the formless mysterious Spirit to manifest through the Human Being, allowing the Authentic Action and Change to take place. The wholistic embodiment of the Non-dual does not take place through repetitive denials of what it isn't, but through the living example of One-duality. To realise and actualise THIS does not require constant negation of the body and mind, but rather acceptance, convergence and integration of *all* dimensions of the Body-Mind-Spirit being.

Like the 'Mountain of Awareness' we looked at in chapter 5, we only see from where we are, or the environment or dimension you identify with in any given moment. If you see from the mego, all appears separate. If 'you' dissolve into Awareness, even for a moment, then all is realised to be the inseparable YOU or SELF. And yet if you see duality and Non-duality as complimentary, you transcend all previous notions of identity and non-identity, and live your life in equanimity as a wholistic Human Being. The Human and the Being exist in harmony. Then there is no negation of what THIS is not, but the grounded acceptance of multiplicity and the One-fused living consciousness which is paradoxically Universal yet Individual. THIS is One-duality, the inseparable, simultaneous presence of anonymous Universal Awareness and Individuality, the consciousness of awakening to the presence of the Soul while here on Earth. It is THIS which is the catalyst for Action and Change in the world, and the route to revealing the Love and Peace at *our* core.

10

∞ The Grounding & Integration of Awareness ∞

Awareness, the SELF, pure Consciousness or Spirit is both the core and ever-present substance of all that *IS*, but THIS is not the end of the human experience. As there is no beginning to THIS, neither is there an ending. Only the polaric mind seeks closure.

As the bare truth of Non-duality is only apparent when subject and object emerge as the inseparable One, the way to reveal THIS is by being still on all levels of being. In the depths of that stillness, nothing appears in consciousness, and yet everything is present. Then, as the mind and senses re-engage, you become aware of Intelligent Love and Peace of Mind (*Being-Consciousness-Bliss*) as duality comes into play. Without duality, nothing could be shared by no one with nobody.

What naturally unfolds from the Non-dual experience is the grounding and integration of THIS in consciousness. It's a bit like having a mind-blowing experience, and then 'returning to Earth' realising it has changed you for good. Your consciousness has shifted from individual to Universal, but it hasn't yet stabilised and grounded, for it is still coming to terms with the 'experience' of Oneness and the Absolute. From a direct experience of the Universal you know beyond doubt that YOU are THIS, and so is everyone and everything else. You cannot deny THIS, and you have no reason to. There is no seeking, and no impulse to look. When the seeker realises they are everything, there is no other to find or become. Now the individual, the world and the universe appear as the illusory dream of form. This may not be a great help if you need to drive a car or go shopping!

In the slower, denser physical dimension of matter, appearance and solidity is constructed from atoms and the forces between atoms. If the vehicle you are travelling in is hit by an out of control lorry, then there will be physical repercussions. The finite bodies of the car and your physical body cannot escape the dimensional consequences. Awareness on the other hand, is infinite and in a sense cannot relate to this event, for these atoms hitting atoms are duality acted out through the physical laws of the universe our forms inhabit, forms which from the inseparability of Awareness appear to be an illusion.

Grounding is literally what it says, the 'Earthing' of Non-dual (Universal) consciousness as the One-dual (Unividual). It is a subtle shift in consciousness wherein the physical becomes a conscious attribute of THIS. Individual or Universal alone are realised as incomplete in the actualisation of the Soul persona on Earth.

We cannot really 'remember' Awareness, because the Real Non-dual experience takes place outside of time and space. It is not recalled through memory, simply recognised as the embedded sweet perfume of Life. The grounding takes place because you are bringing THIS which was uncovered beyond the physical senses, back into the comprehension of those senses, the Being into the consciousness of the Human, and the formless into form. In this way, Awareness is seen and felt to permeate all dimensions of being without negation of any aspect of whom or what we are. In the densest state THIS manifests in the form of the physical body. THIS in its least dense state is pure Consciousness or Awareness. They are not different. It is the least dense state which underlies and permeates all states. When the idea 'I've got it' or 'I am awakened' is let go, the Universal absorption or grounding in consciousness brings about a living equilibrium, and the realisation that You are awakening to the presence of your Soul.

Grounding Awareness is also a process of reprogramming, a re-patterning which includes the nervous and endocrine systems. It takes time to embody the timeless in the time-bound dimension of matter. No part is overlooked, for it becomes clear that Awareness is Spirit. Life is Intelligent beyond our comprehension. If you were brought into life to solely identify with formlessness alone, you wouldn't have been born in a body, and wouldn't be here right now learning to experience THIS in all dimensions of being. To identify with Awareness alone, and to see all other dimensions as illusory, belies the actualisation of Wholeness, lacks Divine humility and negates the existence of the Soul.

THIS in you is not about perfection or imperfection, but that which organically occurs through the acceptance of all You are. It is a three step process of recognition, realisation and actualisation. The mego is surrendered, Awareness *IS*, and, if we continue letting go, the Soul is actualised.

Soulutions

Your Soul is *your* Soul. It is not mine, and yet they consciously share the One essential Divine Spirit. They are family. They are simultaneously separate yet inseparable. They are integral and unique. They are not one and the same but two and the same! A Soul is beyond ideas or logic. Like the atom, it is both dual and Non-dual, for it arises from the recognition and convergence of the two from the One. In Soulness, You live duality and Non-duality as interdependent and complimentary, without attachment or preference. The Unividual is conscious that it is a part and a Whole, or a Whole-part. THIS is the homogenised truth of One-duality, and the natural emergence of the consciousness of the Soul.

The momentum of the Soul is embodied through sharing. Sharing is an aspect of every Soul's consciousness because each Soul recognises its inseparability from the coreless core. Again, Soul with a capital 'S' signifies the awakening consciousness of the Unividual, and not the once dormant or sub-conscious megoic soul. The Soul is conscious it is a Whole-part, and that the same applies to all other versions or appearances. In order to grow, share and express THIS which it is, the sacred expression of One-duality comes into play.

From a profound Universal experience, identity is so radically changed, that the grounding of Awareness takes time to settle in one's consciousness. The grounding and embodiment of THIS Awareness leads to transparency, healing and growth. That growth is a unique pathway the consciousness of the Soul follows without judgement or preference because it is the Divine impulse of the Heart Stream of Consciousness, the flow of Universal Intelligence. The Soul realises it is divinity without having to be *the* Divine, a quality which can be described as Divine humility. As the grounding continues, you may well end up doing something in the world you might never have imagined possible. You are now no longer fighting to get to the non-idea of the SELF, but flowing downstream in the current of the One Life, in the knowingness that THIS is the unfolding of You, the living presence of your Authentic Soul. THIS is a practical engaged spirituality.

To conceptualise THIS will always fall short of the truth, for the recognition and grounding of Awareness requires time, thought, action of mind and expression through One-duality. Any written or spoken word arises from Awareness. Awareness is not the words, and yet words arising from Awareness are traces of THIS. The emergence of the presence of the Soul allows you to experience Unividual multidimensional being, a consciousness that is One-dual. Beyond the confines of duality lies Non-duality. From the Soulless blanket of Non-duality emerges the One-dual Soul, which is You. So, you refers to the mego, YOU to (Universal) Awareness and You to the Unividual Soul.

One way to look at THIS interwoven mystery is through the eyes of the acorn. Let's imagine an acorn is hanging near the end of a branch, looking out at life and a number of other acorns. Only seeing a few feet ahead, it can make out there are other acorns, other leaves and branches, but it cannot see the tree because it cannot turn around. One day, when the conditions are just right, it breaks free falling to the ground with a bump and looks around, seeing that it was just one of thousands of perfect acorns, all attached to the same mighty oak tree. In time, the acorn becomes embedded in the earth. Not resisting the forces and flow of Nature, the acorn finds itself pushing out of the ground and looking around. Only then does the acorn, who was once attached to the tree, and who then fell to the ground, realise that it is no longer an acorn after all, but a tiny oak tree in a forest surrounded by thousands of oak trees at various stages of growth. Is there a more important stage? Is the acorn less than the mighty oak? THIS is in all forms but doesn't deny expression at any stage of being.

In its impulse to share the Peace and Love known to be the Universal core, the Unividual Soul flows with Life conscious that essence and substance are the Non-dual One. There is Non-duality and duality and yet neither are held or identified with, for THIS is free to be all aspects, including a Soul. THIS is One-duality.

> *The Divine is in his essence is infinite and his manifestation too is multitudinously infinite. If that is so, it is not likely that our true integral perfection in being and in nature can come by one kind of realisation alone; it must combine many different strands of divine experience. It cannot be reached by the exclusive pursuit of a single line of identity till that is raised to its absolute; it must harmonise many aspects of the Infinite. An integral consciousness with a multiform dynamic experience is essential for the complete transformation of our nature.*

Sri Aurobindo – The Synthesis of Yoga (p. 114).

Through the grounding and convergence of knowledge and direct experience, THIS reveals the presence of the awakening

Soul, a transcendent step. It is now clear that seeing and being Awareness is part of the evolutionary journey in consciousness, a Universal catalyst supporting the transition and organic movement from Body to Mind to Soul to Spirit. Each new stage includes, converges with, and transcends all previous experience and understandings – for it is only THIS which allows us to truly evolve as human beings.

A glimpse of Awareness and a glimpse of Divine Spirit is One and the same. Here, now, in 2015 humanity is coming out of the mego-based identity, and entering the dimension of the Soul. Awareness is the catalyst moving us from a mego-based consciousness to a Soul-based one. It is only from realising the Soul's absenteeism in the anonymity of Awareness that Unividual consciousness emerges to live its Authentic presence. Surrender takes us to purification and negation which leads to integration.

The evolutionary dimension of Soulness requires the meeting and convergence of Mind and Spirit otherwise the Unividual reality remains as the sub-conscious dormant soul. The individual experience of the Universal is not brought about so that you can be the Absolute, but so that you can recognise and accept the wholistic truth of who and what You are. It is duality which leads to Non-duality which leads to One-duality. And it is the anonymous YOU which reveals the living active You in consciousness and the world. For the Non-dual is something YOU already and always are, not something to reach or become.

The grounding and integration of THIS reveals the next evolutionary step in human consciousness. We are far, far away from being an 'awakened' race of beings, but we are beginning to understand the many connected dimensions of consciousness, and the Sole Cosmic Constant of *our* One inseparable Essence. In truth, we are children of the Universe, just about to take our first steps as Souls in the Universe. We are babies in terms of conscious evolution, but the possibilities remain infinite. THIS is not in our hands to forcefully apply, and yet we are all conscious parts of its manifestation through the actualisation of the One-dual Soul. It is not what is decided by the personality of the human, but Being which flows unobstructed through the Soul's amenable persona.

Being an Authentic Human requires Conscious Living. Conscious Living means living life in the Heart Stream of Consciousness, being open and available to be moved by the impulse of Life itself. THIS impulse of Universal Intelligence is present in human consciousness because the primary qualities of all Being are Intelligent Love and Peace of Mind. These are qualities we all seek, and we seek them because they are the primary sensing of the One mysterious Absolute Spirit we all share.

The Whole picture...

If we continue to live THIS, without limiting possibilities, and not returning to the limitations of mind-based beliefs and restrictions, then the grounding becomes increasingly stabilised and embodied. THIS is seen to be You without division, the dual and the Non-dual without denial or negation. Then the natural flow of the Intelligence of Life, the Heart Stream of Consciousness, initiates cycles of Action and Change through You. THIS is the sharing and expression only Unividuality can bring. The Aristotelian logic of polaric thought has given way to a naturally emerging wholism.

To look at an example of the Whole, let's imagine that you are water, and pose the question 'What is the reality of water?' – is it:

A. A visible liquid or
B. An invisible gas (vapour)

There are many answers all part of the One truth which interweaves them. The Whole is many parts, and the parts are the One Whole. The answer has many more responses than the polaric mind can initially see:

Answer 1: A – Because it's experienced as a visible liquid and 'flows', it must be a liquid.

Answer 2: B – Because it's experienced as a formless invisible vapour, the visible A is unreal.

Answer 3: A and B – water is experienced as liquid and gas, visible and invisible so it is both A and B.

Answer 4: Water is experienced as neither A nor B – but as the yet unmentioned 'solid' form of ice (C).

Answer 5: Water is liquid, gas and solid, depending on the dimension it appears in, so the answer is now all three, A, B and C.

Or, put another way, it's a bit like seeing life from the viewpoint of a droplet of rain.

I fall through the sky. I am liquid rain. I strike the Earth and enter the mountain stream. I am no longer the droplet, but the stream. The stream reaches the powerful river. I am the river. The river reaches the ocean. I am the ocean. The ocean freezes. I am solid ice. As the ocean surface heats up, the ice melts and evaporates. I am formless vapour. As the vapour cools and condenses, it eventually forms clouds. I am visible yet formless cloud. Then the infinite cycle begins again, as the droplet falls from the cloud. I am rain once more. This seemingly ever-changing reality has several consistencies throughout:

1. The movement and appearance from liquid to solid to gas are *all* real.
2. Water has many faces, but is equally 'itself' in all dimensions; liquid, gas and solid.

The fuller picture is understood through the knowledge and acceptance of all frequencies or dimensions. Now which is the true picture of water? The whole understanding of what water 'really' is doesn't come from negation or denial of any 'other' form or formlessness. Water *is*, and our acceptance of the many guises is the key to understanding its multiplicity in forms and non-forms. Likewise, to live and experience Wholeness, one must let go of each and every assumption of what the Whole is. When *all* preferences are let go, Truth appears, and the Whole is known and lived. The Whole allows us to live aligned and interwoven with Universal Life, and it is THIS which is the pathway to a naturally unfolding human evolution.

As the integration of THIS continues, human consciousness increasingly lives an Authentic consistency. Because there is no clinging physically, emotionally, mentally or spiritually to the truth of your being, You are truly free to experience the wonder of Life. It is not that you are Spirit or not Spirit. YOU are Spirit and You are filled with Spirit. There's no need to debate THIS. Now you are temporary and infinite, everything and nothing. Now it is clear there is a part of you that will die, an eternal YOU which is, was and will always be, and You, human consciousness awakening to the presence of Soul, which knows both these to be true. As to what is Real? The acorn and the oak reveal THIS. You cannot be one without being the other. All is THIS. THIS is All.

Being is the indivisible singularity of what YOU are, what we all are, and what all IS. In awakening to Soulness, there's a unified acceptance that You are formless Being, in the form of Human expression. A Unividual awakening to the consciousness of the Soul is the unique human conscious expression of the indivisible and interconnected Whole. In THIS there is acceptance, Peace and Love. Now you are perfect and imperfect, Universal and Individual, dual and Non-dual, of form and yet formless. THIS is who You are.

Now there is no following of personal or societal expectations. Life is lived from an organic compassion and integrity in harmony with the Heart Stream of Consciousness. Be still, and know THIS.

11

∞ The Sacredness of Duality ∞

THIS is always present and always experienced. The integral pulse of Life is that which leads to, encapsulates and expresses the living Whole. THIS – experienced as the stillness of our Non-dual founding Reality, is brought to life in the Unividual through the sacred impulse of recognition, realisation and actualisation.

The consciousness of awakening to the presence of the Soul is a balanced acceptance of the Body-Mind-Spirit triad, for it is THIS which allows life to be lived as a Human Being conscious of the Sole Cosmic Constant while experiencing the multidimensional reality. If any form of consciousness is based on denial or exclusivity of any part, it is incomplete and lacking the presence of Love and Peace flowing from *our* core.

Someone who lives in the mego denies the existence of the Non-dual foundation. Someone who absolutely identifies with the idea of Awareness dismisses the blossoming interplay of duality and the value of Authentic worldly Action through the consciousness of the Soul. It's clear that there is negation or denial in both the mego and the conceptualisation of the non-mego, for they deny the very existence of each other. One-duality is the solid yet flexible crystallisation of human consciousness, the paradoxical living of self and SELF in Authenticity.

Duality is sacred. Non-duality is sacred. They are the two fundamental principles of existence, one active, the other passive. Without the active participation of these two principles, there would be no Universe and no Earth. What took place from the *'Initial Singularity'* and the Big Bang, created the Universe. Particles and anti-particles, two opposing charges converged to reveal existence. So from the very beginning, duality was in play to express the infinite possibilities of the One Universal Life.

Without the functioning of duality the Cosmos would not exist. Without participating in duality, you could not fall in love with another and experience the dualistic interchange of THIS. All existence, including duality, is sacred. Have compassion for the driven personality of the mego, for without its presence you would have no desire to escape it and find the true persona of your Soul.

To be absolutely clear, I'm not referring to the mego's version of duality, which is a self-absorbed, self-centred 'it's all about me' materialistic divisive mentality, but to an all-inclusive consciousness which is refined, evolving ever-closer to the core qualities of Love and Peace. THIS is One-duality, human consciousness wherein the Universal is lived, shared and expressed through the Unividuality of the Soul.

Anyone home?

The common misconception is to believe that we should rid ourselves of individual identity or 'the person'. This again is only a partial truth. To experience the Love and Peace of what we *all* are, it is true, you will need to let go of your supposed identity, and yet from this timeless experience the blossoming of consciousness continues. The meeting with, or temporary dissolution in Awareness is a stepping stone, for it purifies the mego, and the individualised version of mind is seen through and transcended. And, once THIS is grounded in consciousness, the Universal-Individual or Unividual manifests. So it is not through negation, but rather through acceptance and transmutation that awakening to the presence of the Soul is realised.

The disintegration and purging of the mego does not mean that individuality dies too. In the true Non-dual experience, the individual appears to be an illusory dream, but once THIS is grounded and integrated back in the dimension of the physical world, then a Universal-Individual Authentic 'me' emerges. THIS is a 'me' because You have experienced, accepted and understood the nature of a combined uniqueness and inseparable inclusivity. It is through the transcendence of the individual identity and Universal non-identity of Awareness that THIS is grounded in an evolving, dynamic and radical consciousness. It is through THIS that Change and Action for the Whole take place in the world. Awareness purges the personality of the mego so that the Soul may live the Authentic persona in the world.

It is refreshing and liberating to look at a sunset, knowing that THIS is the indivisible One, the seeing itself, and the sharing of the experience too. The doorway to Non-duality is through duality. The Soul's experience is one of non-negation, and of openness to all dimensions. So although the sunset is known to be YOU, the loving, empathic and compassionate qualities of duality are experienced too. Without the dualistic gateway of the human senses, Oneness would not appear, and Awareness could not be experienced as the foundational Reality it really is.

If you really want to learn and grow, then go out into nature and find somewhere to immerse yourself. Take no distractions, no pen or paper and just find a quiet spot. If you sit there long enough, you will begin to see, really see. You will begin to hear and really hear. Look at how THIS wonderful creation is a play of dualities, the play of the One as the many. When you are ready, the mind will reveal that YOU are the One. There is no difference between YOU and the tree, or YOU and the Universe. And yet there is a unique You present who realises THIS, for not everyone is conscious of THIS simultaneously. So it is duality which allows us to experience Non-duality.

As THIS becomes balanced and stabilised, so does the deepening sense of Unividuality. The consciousness of the Soul, which is paradoxical, converges with all versions of THIS. There is only One, yet there is a one who knows and lives THIS. There is no separate conditioned personality appearing as the foreground of consciousness, and yet there is an interconnected persona, an Authentic Soul which arises from the direct experience and knowledge of Universal anonymity.

THIS is a sharing of the Universal we all are, and any sharing requires duality. To share the One is therefore most clearly expressed as One-duality. THIS is the founding nature of the Soul, how awakening appears as the foreground of Unividual consciousness, and the root and reason of the Change and Action it manifests. And in that play of Life, the 'good' and the 'bad' rub together. Life, the Universe and human evolution emerge, live and depend on such meetings and reactions, because for each cause there is a corresponding effect.

When you act from fear, you share fear, and an Act of Love creates a corresponding sense of Love. When fear meets Authentic Love, fear disintegrates, and yet when Love meets fear, our sense of Love expands. This is because Love is a primary quality of Being, and the ever-expanding truth of our evolution. Fear will never overcome Love, for THIS is our core, our reality and our destination.

One-duality is sacred because it is the conscious sharing of the Universal One. From the One come the interconnected many, and the Unividual Soul is one of the many who is a conscious manifestation of the One. If your understanding is still that there is 'nobody here' in your consciousness, then you are identifying with the idea of Awareness, which means you are negating the natural multiplicity of the Universe, and the true all-inclusiveness of Being. By clinging to the experience or hanging on to an intellectual understanding, you deny awakening to the presence of your Soul.

THIS covered over by neglect is the individual mego.

THIS in the vibrant stillness of Non-duality is the anonymous Awareness of the Universal SELF.

THIS beyond the dual and the Non-dual is the Unividual Soul.

If you are the parent of a child or children, you will recognise the loving, sacred value of duality. To look into the eyes of your newly born child and to appreciate the similarities *and* the differences is a miracle of life which is transformative and unforgettable. There is a sharing. If there is no duality, there is no momentum, no spark, no exchange and flow, no dynamism. For darkness to be seen, we need light, for the mego self to evolve, we need to realise the non-mego, and for THIS to manifest in the world, it requires awakening to all dimensions of being.

The Soul who knows THIS Awareness is looking through these eyes, a You that is Universal yet Individual, and a You establishing Action and Change in the world. Because they are Authentic, these Actions and Changes will always benefit You and the Whole. Not one or the other, but both together.

One-duality is how we recognise the appearance of the world as a beautiful collective, while simultaneously knowing that Oneness is here and now, always. You have a consciousness endowed with the knowingness that your Soul is no less and no more than another's, that You are the same but different. You are the same essential SELF appearing as the part which knows it is Whole. The Whole-part.

Everything is One because it emanates from the One Source, not because we are identical in all dimensions of being. How pointless that would be. One-duality is the conscious experiencing of the SELF across and within all dimensions. When you lose the separate person in Awareness, then the window of awakening to the Soul opens. If you stay with Awareness as the not-you of non-identity, you cling to the *idea* of *your* experience, holding on rather than letting go and Living THIS. There is no need to become Awareness. YOU are Awareness. So share THIS as only You can. It is THIS all-inclusive sense of Love which shares and unifies.

The contribution the Soul makes is not an idea, an invention or an intention centred on self-benefit, but naturally arising and intuited wholistic Actions and Changes which feed and nourish the Whole. For instance, I can ask myself what is the point of writing this book. The primary reason for writing THIS is to share the persona of my Soul and encourage you to do the same. It is THIS freedom which if we practise readily and openly, will support the healing of the world, and the freeing up of evolutionary possibilities. Committing THIS to paper brings clarity and understanding which although already alive in consciousness, has yet to appear in the world. Writing this book is the solidifying of learning and experience. When you Act from the Soul, it is sensed and felt throughout your entire being that what you are doing is also the reason for being here.

One of my favourite pastimes is to listen to music while writing. But it has to be a certain type of music. Soul music. It's not about a specific era, or any particular style or what somebody like 'me' should like, but music which really speaks, sharing the Soul of another. Though these pieces of music are mostly instrumental, they all 'speak' volumes. They all share. From the divine infused works of George Handel to the fragile but powerful honesty of contemporary singer-songwriter James Bay.

What music does THIS for You? Why? When? How?

The difference between the personality of the mego and the persona of the Unividual Soul shows how and why One-duality works. The mego is confined to having, grasping and attaining for itself alone, thereby increasing division and separation. The persona of the Soul is unconfined and open to creativity, sharing and expression, awakening in consciousness when the personal and Universal are two and the same, and the limitations of polaric thought have become transparent. From a separate 'me' personality of the mego to the 'no me' non-personality of the SELF to the 'me' and 'not me' of the Authentic Soul's persona, duality returns purified and shining from the One Source. There is meaning and Intelligence behind and within all Life, and THIS is brought into the world by You awakening to the presence of your Soul. There is an 'I' which lies beyond ideas of separation and the inseparable. It is the Whole-part. It is You, consciousness awakening to the living presence of the Soul walking the Earth.

In One-duality there is no negation. The thought of how one must be or how one should act are seen through. If THIS is limited to an intellectual explanation of the perfection of emptiness, then the Wholeness it purportedly represents is paradoxically Spiritless. It is possible for You to take part in Change and Action, for THIS arises from the awakening to Soulness. That is why for You to be a conscious expression of THIS, the dual and Non-dual ideas and experiences must be let go. Only then is consciousness free to be You.

The duality of creativity is another important area of One-duality. Without the creative flux, the duality of imagination, and the expansion of consciousness, we would not have been inspired and uplifted to Act by 'others':

Don't be satisfied with stories, how things have gone with others.
Unfold your own myth.
– Rumi

The painter has the Universe in his mind and hands.
– Leonardo da Vinci

What keeps life fascinating is the constant creativity of the soul.
– Deepak Chopra

All these quotes share the creative dynamism of One-duality, as they each express awakening to the expression and creativity of the Soul.

The true art of creation takes place when the individual is lost in the Universal, and returns with a co-creation from the sharing which has taken place. That's why you lose all track of time when you are in the creative 'zone'. You are lost in Intelligent Love. You have effectively transcended time, albeit for a while. When THIS exchange is shared with others, it represents an Authentic reminder of our interconnectedness and the unified relationship we all share.

From One-duality there is the manifestation of Unividual Action. There is the recognition that there is nothing I can change personally, for the 'personal' has been transformed, and yet there is Change which arises in and from the persona. Action and Change is inevitable. In the flow of Life it is unavoidable. As the grub to chrysalis to butterfly metamorphosis shows us, Nature is an on-going expression of THIS.

Likewise there is the recognition of One-duality. It is the Authentic expression of the multiplicity of the One, creating Action from Being, not the doing of the mego. There is an 'I' but it is an 'I' which exists as a part and Whole, a Unividual persona conscious of the layers and dimensions of Being. The Soul is One-dual because it is inseparable yet conscious of the dual flow of the One. The 'I' has responsibility, a common collective responsibility, for it is all of 'ours'. Just as there is a world which is ours, not 'personally' mine. These are not thoughts or 'nice' ideas; they are simply what appears in awakening to the presence of the Soul.

One-duality brings about a humbling recognition that You are Spirit, here in the form of a body and mind, no longer the dozing or partially conscious soul, but an awakening consciousness which knows itself to be an integral part of the One Life.

Here, now in 2015, we are awakening to Soulness, the unstoppable tide of Wholeness which is sweeping the globe. THIS is bringing about Action and Change in the world, and catalysing the metamorphosis from individual to Unividual consciousness. As these words are mine and not mine, they are simply the expression and sharing of THIS.

You are here in human form for good reason, to experience the physical and mental dimensions of Being, and when you are ready and willing, to remember your formlessness. When you have accepted and grounded the formless YOU, then the persona of the Soul is free to appear as the foreground of consciousness.

To be conscious of the dualities of mind and body doesn't mean that we don't realise our Non-dual Oneness. Only the conditioning of polaric thought demands absolute identification with one *or* the other. That's because in polaric thinking, they are perceived as different, as opposites, as one being real and the other unreal, when from the Unividual perspective, they are not. They are both real.

If we embrace duality from a Universal perspective, we open ourselves to the emerging Change and Action of Universal Intelligence. To share is a natural consequence of the Love we essentially are. And it is only through THIS sharing that humankind will survive and evolve. You can make a difference, a contribution, for that is why You are here in the world.

12

∞ Change & Action ∞

The consciousness of awakening to the presence of the Soul, or Soulness, is the result of the meeting and convergence of Human and Being. The hybrid consciousness of the finite and Infinite, it is the dynamic impulse of the One living in, and moving through the persona of the Soul, and THIS is the next stepping stone in the evolution of human consciousness.

Action and Change are brought about through the natural flow of the consciousness of the Unividual. These Human functionalities of Being are clearly different to the action and change forced through by the mego which sustain and propagate the illusion of separation. When Soulness stabilises as the foreground of consciousness, we become receptive and alive to the emergence of Change and Action, the Universal processes through which Awareness manifests in the world through You.

I alone cannot change the world, but I can cast a stone across the waters to create many ripples.
– Mother Teresa

As mentioned in the previous chapter, Action and Change are the resulting consequences of being in the flow of the Heart Stream of Consciousness, and not megoic choices based on the divisiveness of personal gain. Indeed, separation in any form, including the self-isolating belief of being an individual, has now been transcended through the meeting and blending of Awareness. Awareness has 'seen' Awareness and merged as the One unified Being.

It reminds me of helping my Mum make wine when I was a kid. If the dense mego is represented by the grapes, the cheesecloth or filter acts in a similar fashion to the transformational effect of Universal recognition, and permits the expression of the juice of the Soul. What was essentially in the mego is also in the Soul, but now consciousness has simplified or purified, and let go of the dense conditioning it once carried and which kept the soul hidden in the depths of the human psyche. Now consciousness is not driven by the mego's separate identity, but finds heart, life and momentum through the actualisation of the Universal.

The idea that there is a need to evolve human consciousness is true. But the fact there is no doer who can do so is also true. So is there really nothing to do? What there is to do is THIS which arises, appears and gets done. Who is this done by? By You. It is clear that Real Transformation comes from the Action of Love and not from some isolated sense of mego. The Soul knows the paradox that it is essentially Love, for it arises from, and exists in, THIS Intelligent Love. However, the Unividual is not attached to being *the* strategist, purpose or doer of the Action, for any Action is intuited and taken for the Whole, which it is inseparable from. And so the Unividual although conscious of the Action, does not identify with the Action as being 'theirs' and just gets on with the task in hand. The Soullessness of Awareness has brought about the actualisation of the Soul's persona.

It's the action, not the fruit of the action, that's important. You have to do the right thing. It may not be in your power, may not be in your time, that there'll be any fruit. But that doesn't mean you stop doing the right thing. You may never know what results come from your action. But if you do nothing, there will be no result.
– Mahatma Gandhi

Authentic Action is not based on personal gain, or designed to overcome or deny, but a natural sharing and expression of what we are at our core. Soul Action is not based on the 'me' or 'us' of a country, religion or group, but on THIS – the all-inclusive Whole.

Change and Action are organic expressions of Spirit and Nature, for they are Universal momentum. They unfold naturally, just as rain falls from a cloud, or as the chrysalis transforms into a butterfly. The word expression comes from the Latin *expressio* – meaning a pressing out, or a coming out of itself. The One coming out of itself into the world is expressed through each and every de-conditioned persona, for it is the dual expression of the Non-dual One.

Then comes the reconciliation of outer and inner purpose: to bring that essence – consciousness – into the world of form and thereby transform the world. The ultimate purpose of that transformation goes far beyond anything the human mind can imagine or comprehend. And yet, on this planet at this time, that transformation is the task allotted to us. That is the reconciliation of inner and outer purpose, the reconciliation of the world and God.
– Eckhart Tolle

Change brings about Action and Action brings about Change, these are infinite active cycles within the Universe. The transformation of human consciousness takes place through sharing the essential qualities of Universal Love and Peace, revealing Change and Action in the world. When human consciousness is disconnected from the core qualities of Intelligent Love and Peace of Mind, the limitless ever-present flow of the Heart Stream of Consciousness is either being repressed, ignored or over-looked. When this disconnection takes place in the individual or world consciousness, we are alienated from our root, and become like lost children lacking focus, looking for remedies and replacements to plug the hole in our hearts and minds. We have forgotten the reality of the Soul. When what is lacking is known and grounded in consciousness, the Divine Intelligence of *Being-Consciousness-Bliss* flows and Change and Action take place through the Unividual.

We are in a time of rebalance, an era of Change and Action. In the early part of the twenty-first century, we are in the initial stages of a step in the evolution of human consciousness which can be described as awakening to the consciousness of the Soul. THIS is the recognition that beneficial, lasting and Authentic Change for the Whole is brought about through embodying the impulse of our essential Oneness.

It will not happen overnight. Change and Action will first take place as an escalating individual to Unividual metamorphosis before it becomes the expanded worldview consciousness. There is not a specific time or event which will make THIS obvious. The old will fall away as the new comes in. Indeed it is already taking place. And You have a role to play in THIS. Not as a mego, not as a 'nobody', but as a Soul walking the Earth. If you can learn to be and express the truth of your Soul, how you will be living and what You will be doing will bring joy and fulfilment to the Whole. In THIS way we can explore the potentials of Consciousness, evolving a 'new' worldview rooted in Love and Peace rather than continuing an animalistic global culture of greed, selfishness, war and fear.

When you get the chance, look up at a cloudless night sky. There are possibly thousands of stars in your view. Through the physicality of the eyes, and the pictures translated by your brain, You are looking from one perspective only. Do you know how many stars exist? Well, recent estimates suggest around 70 sextillion – that's the number seven followed by twenty-two zeros: 70,000,000,000,000,000,000,000. Each star is different in size, shape, composition, temperature, colour, and in the distance they are from the Sun – yet all of them are beautiful stars, as is your Soul. To realise just how vast THIS is, and to put it in perspective, if we shared these stars between every single person on Earth, each of us would have millions and millions of stars. That's an indication of how inconceivably vast the cosmos really is. This One-dual perspective can be used to remind us of Divine humility, while opening our hearts and minds to our infinite cumulative potential. You simply cannot imagine the possibilities, but You can help make them happen.

It is at THIS point in the evolution of human consciousness that we begin to Change and Act for, and with, the Whole. As a Unividual, you are in convergence with the Heart Stream of Consciousness, the flow of the Universe. Not in some ungrounded and deluded way, but in a solid, empowering and functional manner. All lasting Change and Action comes from THIS wholistic interconnection, the convergence of the passive and the active, the Non-dual and the dual, the yin and the yang of One-duality.

When you follow THIS impulse of being a conscious tool for Change and Action, you will not only find enjoyment but fulfilment too. And how will THIS be expressed through You? The more you let go of the idea of what and how, the more space appears in consciousness, and the more what THIS is will become apparent. The paradoxical mystery is that you do not 'decide'. Your acceptance and Surrender to the Divine Intelligence of the Universe is the key to the opening of the floodgates of your Soul, and the path which allows recognition and conscious Action to be realised for the Whole. Aware of the Divine flow of Universal Intelligence, the doubts and fears of the wandering mind fade. You were created with reason and purpose, and THIS is the reason for You being here now.

You will only really know how THIS appears in your life when it is happening. It will stand in its own power, for it will be Authentic and You. You won't be identifying with 'it', just expressing 'it' in whatever shape or form 'it' takes. You will not be primarily motivated by the commercial possibilities, or demotivated by 'personal' criticism, for You will be Acting for the Whole as only You are able. As THIS impulse arises from the core qualities of Divine Being, then Intelligent Love is always present in any such Action. You are nurtured and cared for, and

THIS is always enough. The 'proof' of awakening to Soulness is
that Action takes place in connection with the Whole, and
benefits the Whole – a Whole which includes You.

Authentic worldly Action may not always immediately
appear to be coming from Love and Peace. Here's an example
which comes to mind, from the Old Testament of the Bible:

*¹⁶ One day two women came to King Solomon, ¹⁷ and one of them
said:*

*Your Majesty, this woman and I live in the same house. Not long ago
my baby was born at home, ¹⁸ and three days later her baby was born.
Nobody else was there with us.*

*¹⁹ One night while we were all asleep, she rolled over on her baby,
and he died. ²⁰ Then while I was still asleep, she got up and took my
son out of my bed. She put him in her bed then she put her dead baby
next to me.*

*²¹ In the morning when I got up to feed my son, I saw that he was
dead. But when I looked at him in the light, I knew he wasn't my
son.*

*²² "No!" the other woman shouted. "He was your son. My baby is
alive!"*

"The dead baby is yours," the first woman yelled. "Mine is alive!"

*They argued back and forth in front of Solomon, ²³ until finally he
said, "Both of you say this live baby is yours. ²⁴ Someone bring me a
sword."*

*A sword was brought, and Solomon ordered, ²⁵ "Cut the baby in
half! That way each of you can have part of him."*

*²⁶ "Please don't kill my son," the baby's mother screamed. "Your
Majesty, I love him very much, but give him to her. Just don't kill
him."*

*The other woman shouted, "Go ahead and cut him in half. Then
neither of us will have the baby."*

*²⁷ Solomon said, "Don't kill the baby." Then he pointed to the first
woman, "She is his real mother. Give the baby to her."*

²⁸ Everyone in Israel was amazed when they heard how Solomon had made his decision. They realised that God had given him wisdom to judge fairly.

One woman acted from the mego, and the other from Love. Solomon's Action was from the wisdom of the Soul. Another clue will be that the expression or sharing of an Authentic Action will allow you to keep an open mind to growing and evolving. You will not be the mego convinced it is 'awakened' or 'enlightened', for You are simply awakening to the consciousness of the Soul. You will be learning and experiencing how to be You more deeply, more effectively and more completely as each day goes by. You simply 'flow' more easily with Life as You awaken to Soulness. And it is then the journey really begins.

Actualising You...

By sharing your Soul You enrich and inspire others to touch their deepest and truest sense of being too. THIS Action not only feeds 'others' but nourishes You too. That's Soul magic. When you give, you share the ever-expanding reward. Giving is an Action of the Soul, and not a form of loss as the materialistic-bound mego would presume. To the Unividual, to give *is* to receive. The discernment of when and what You give comes from knowingness, and not from any sense of guilt, societal pressure or any self-orientated scheme designed to return personal benefit. Giving in THIS way, You are more likely to give whole-heartedly, assuredly and without needing to be identified as the giver.

THIS is not about escaping to an ideal future world. THIS is about being You, here and now, and in being You, a natural, fulfilling contribution to the Whole of Life takes place. If you seek to establish *your* idealistic future vision you are discon-necting yourself from THIS. THIS is not about your version, but Your contribution. To a Unividual, the idea of *'which cog am I?'* in the imaginary clock of humanity is irrelevant and not even a question which arises. Although in one sense 'I' appear as a cog, it is the knowing that I am a cog Acting as part of a greater connected Whole which provides the sense of joy, peace and fulfilment. An isolated part is not conscious of the existence of the Whole, and the identified Whole cannot distinguish the existence of the many parts. I am both part and Whole simultaneously, a Whole-part, the consciousness of the Soul.

If there was no role for duality in human consciousness, then there would be no exchange, and no interchange. There would be no one reading and no one writing. Life would be pointless, hollow and void, and lacking in human spirit, endeavour, connection and expression. The Act of sharing THIS is the dualism of the anonymous Non-dual One, and in this sense, it is the manifestation of the evolutionary pulse, and One-duality.

THIS does not concern ideals or opinions, for it is simply about being You. Change and Action are always ours, always THIS. Nothing from Change or Action will ever truly belong to you. There is no separate you any longer for it to come from or to belong to. It is no longer personal preference, but Action from the persona of the Soul revealing Universal Intelligence in the world of form. Change and Action arise from the Heart of Being, and carry a power which is transformative, beneficial, inspiring and life-changing. The Soul's nature is to share THIS.

One thing I have realised is that if you look back over your life, there are clues scattered about if you look carefully without pre-determining what you will find. Inevitably, Change and Action are from the Soul, and are something which flow from, with, and connect to, the Love and Peace of essential Being. In short, what You 'do' will be something from Love. If it is something from Love, You will wholeheartedly give your time and energy without taking it personally, and have no need to constantly seek attention, praise and recognition. You will love what You do, so You will give and receive simultaneously. You will realise that THIS is simply how You express and share Love in the world, a Love which expresses the integral Oneness of Life, while at the same time being a unique complement to the Whole.

Like the stars in the Universe, there are innumerable possibilities of what You can be and do in the world, so why construct a fake version of what THIS is in your mind? Be Your Self. Each Soul has a unique 'song' and it is THIS which benefits the Whole. It may be that you are a great Mother or Father who does a fantastic job supporting your family. Perhaps you make chairs, or write for the local newspaper, or maybe You grow and share the most delicious vegetables. Whatever it is, it will be an embodiment of the Soul, and exemplify who You are. You will not need praise and societal acceptance that THIS is something 'special' or 'worthwhile' for the underlying peace and loving nature of it will reveal its true power. It is simply the Authentic blending of what You do and who You are, and with the power of Love, you'll give it everything You have and more.

Whatever You do from Soulness will be recognisable. Action from the Soul will be unique and contain Authentic qualities. You will not be copying another, or carrying out a specific role to 'look good' or to make money. You will be doing it because it's true to You. It will be done from Love, and THIS is how You experience and express THIS Love. It has Universal reason and purpose, for it is the earthly expression of all You are.

Finding or realising what THIS is cannot be forced or rushed, and will only appear when You are ready, open and available. You will sense its multidimensional value. You will do 'it' to the best of your ability, because you will love what You are doing. You will love what You are doing because You will know it to be connected to the Whole, as You are. If 'it' is really Authentic, You will not be able to trace a specific 'doer' or point to the individual you, for the very idea of 'who is the doer' will no longer arise. And neither will there be a need to enquire or know the answer.

When You are present, then You are in the flow of Life, the Heart Stream of Consciousness, and such questions have no relevance, for You are being true to the flow of Universal Intelligence, and Acting from the consciousness of your Soul.

Now the Universal is shared through the Individual without separation. There is no dilemma, for the Individual has undergone Change and transformation, and is no longer the same megoic personality but a living wholistic consciousness. Even the preference to identify or non-identify with one or the other no longer arises. You are in the world, and not in the world. You are Universal and Individual. There is no negation or denial of who You are. THIS is the all-accepting, all-embracing reality of Soulness, an endless beginning, and THIS is the consciousness of the Unividual persona.

13

∞ The Unividual ∞

The Universal-Individual or Unividual is the next stepping stone in the evolution of human consciousness. As the integral consciousness aware of the Body, Mind, Spirit triad, it is accompanied by the knowingness that You are awakening to the presence of your Soul.

The word 'Individual' most commonly means 'a single human being' yet it is derived from the Latin *indīviduālis,* meaning 'indivisible'. So, what is an individual indivisible from? In the isolated mind of the mego, it is the belief in a completely separate self. From the Soul's perspective, it is unique, alive to all dimensions, and indivisible from the Whole.

The word 'Universal' means 'characteristic of the whole' and is derived from the Latin *ūniversālis,* meaning 'of the universe'. The word Whole is our focus here, not the idea of limiting existence to the confines of any universe or universes.

So the word 'Unividual' suggests an Authentic persona, a 'who' indivisible from the anonymous 'what' of Awareness. THIS is Oneness emerging through the presence of You, for they converge and crystallise to reveal a living, breathing multidimensional being.

The process of the evolution of human consciousness as outlined in this book has moved from the separate part to the Universal Whole, before THIS is grounded in consciousness and the Unividual blooms as a conscious Whole-part. The wholistic mind of the Unividual goes beyond the individual mind limited by duality and the anonymous no-mind of Non-duality. It is THIS One-dual consciousness which sees and incorporates all dimensions of human being-ness, and is accompanied by the knowingness that the mego's recognition and transformation by the Universal experience of Being is only a stepping stone, not a conclusive finality. It is an ending in the sense that the mego is exposed and one's identity with separation falls away, but there is no claim to having completed all there is, or having arrived at some 'awakened' finality. There is no need or requirement, for You know, You feel, You sense, that THIS awakening going on here and now is the living convergence of inner and outer Being, and it is THIS which remains undeniable to the Unividual. Unividuality naturally compounds the root, persona, integrity and expression of human consciousness. It does not deny or exclude any part; any dimension of being or Being itself, for it is the Whole-part. It is Human consciousness grounded in the world yet interconnected with the formlessness of Being. In this sense it is the consciousness which makes 'Doing' conscious, because for the Unividual, 'Doing' arises from and through the Ground of Being itself.

When we are Doing from Being, it is Authentic Doing and not the unconscious disconnected doing of the mego. Authentic Doing is a window through which Consciousness is expressed in the world. When You are in harmony with the Heart Stream of Consciousness, You manifest Universal Intelligence. THIS allows for Change, Action and Doing which are all expressions of Being in the world of form. As human consciousness continues to evolve, any future world will be decided by our ability to share THIS Unividual reality.

It is not the uniqueness of the persona and individual expression which creates war and destruction, but discordant megoic action which takes place when we remain ignorant of our underlying Universality. Or to put it another way, it is not the persona that's the problem, but the egoism which exists when human consciousness is bound by the idea that 'I' am completely separate, which only feeds the 'us' and 'them' rationale of politics, religions and beliefs.

A Unividual has simultaneous comprehension of the finite

and Infinite, for it is Universal Being living a unique persona. THIS multidimensional Mind, Body, Spirit reality is the realisation and awareness of Oneness in diversity, of the formless present in all forms, with each Soul a conscious Whole-part.

Now it is clear that the mego was the stepping stone to the Universal, and the recognition of the Universal was the faceless mirror to awakening the presence of the Unividual Soul. Without the mego, beginning the journey would have been impossible. Each step is part of the ever-unfolding Whole. And yet now, there is the emergence of an Authentic persona, one which lives as, and is held, nourished and steered by the inseparability of Oneness. It is not confined to duality and separation. It is not a blanket vision which depersonalises 'other' appearances of THIS. *All* is THIS, and it is the transparency of Love and Peace which interconnect the parts and the Whole.

So, the Unividual sees and senses the separate and the inseparable, and naturally flows with the Heart Stream of Consciousness. Form and formlessness are now so interwoven in one's being that the Unividual is conscious of his or her embodiment, conscious of a body and a persona being lived in space and time, conscious of subjectivity, yet simultaneously conscious that all 'parts' are Universal and in an Absolute sense, not separate at all. Everything is One, and yet from the One comes duality, the faculty and expression of sharing, the symbiosis of duality and Non-duality, and the window to unknown potentials. THIS is a paradox. You are the One living in and as the multiplicity of the world, for such is the reality of awakening to the presence of the Soul.

Look at the Sun. It naturally explodes and expresses. It is a ball of energy in a constant flux of Action and Change. It warms the planet, drives the hydrologic cycle, and makes life on Earth possible. THIS is the Act of sharing present in Universal Intelligence. THIS sharing of energy is not only the nature of the Soul, but the nature of the entire Universe.

The Soul has no requirement to 'become' or to seek identification with Awareness, for it is already conscious that it is. THIS is the ocean knowing that in the dimension of form and expression, it is a wave, and the wave knowing that it is, and can only ever be, the ocean. The expression of the wave comes and goes, while knowing the ocean is always present. In knowing that unique expression and inseparability are both realities of the Soul, it is free to live and be. THIS is the paradoxical nature of the One-dual Soul.

Now 'I' look at the view in the back garden knowing that THIS is Whole, that 'I' am recognisable in unbroken interconnected parts and a multi-formed Oneness. There is no need to seek or identify with Essence, for Essence *IS*, here, now and always. THIS is an evolutionary consciousness, the veritable freedom of a Whole Human without yearning or seeking any 'other', and the natural unfolding of Universal Intelligence.

It is Change and Action which feed, support and encourage the natural expression of the Unividual. These expressions call out to us all, opening a window to the living knowledge that we are parts of the One human family, the One indivisible Life. You are not simply 'nobody' with 'nothing to say' and 'nothing to do', for the One-dual Unividual is a vital, living, dynamic consciousness alive to all dimensions of being.

Whereas, once upon a time nothing was seen to be 'bad' – now You sense that anything which destroys and undermines connection and unity is divisive and out of 'sync' with the Heart Stream of Consciousness. It's not so much that it's 'bad' but that it's the unconscious divisive action of the mego. Words which are spoken and not lived are hollow and lacking the Soul's Authenticity. THIS is a new and transparent worldview consciousness in which each of us may participate wholeheartedly for the benefit of all humanity and all Life.

The old ways of the megoic world are breaking down as Unividuality emerges as the foreground in consciousness. For millennia there have been examples that a new species was on the horizon. Now, it is here in ever-increasing numbers, as every single day more and more people participate in THIS evolutionary impulse, evolving humankind from Homo sapiens sapiens to Homo Novus or 'New Human'. It is embedded in us all to grow, expand and share with one another for the benefit of the Whole. So even if it appears that there is nothing to be done, there's plenty of Doing going on.

You are part of the awakening of human consciousness, and the task at hand is to embody THIS as You. The world does not need copies, but originals, the true You. Strange as it may seem, the contribution to the Whole by one Authentic You gives far more than a deliberate copy of a Gandhi or a Ramana Maharshi. You are not Gandhi or Ramana, for You are a Unividual capable of your very own contribution to *our* evolution. The beautiful truth here is that each Soul *lives* that contribution. It is not something to plan, but the expression which comes to light from the Change and Action You consciously share as a Unividual.

Everybody can be great because anybody can serve... You only need a heart full of grace and soul generated by love.
– Martin Luther King

THIS evolutionary momentum is not based on animalistic survival, but from the Love we intrinsically share with all life, the foundation, presence and expression of Universal Intelligence. This Love includes *all* forms of Life. We realise that how we are in THIS moment predicts what we will become, and the type of world our children's children will one day inherit.

You can manifest Change and Action. For THIS to occur, it must arise from that which binds us together, the Oneness we both share and are, for Authentic Transformation only comes from Intelligent Love. THIS point in human evolution is a time for You to express, create, share and consciously participate in the healing and renewal of human consciousness. In that way You are open and available to share and receive. THIS is not a new religion, nor is it ambitious idealism, simply the recognition that in order to approach and establish Unity, there must be parts which converge to exemplify and live THIS Unity.

A Unividual is not by any means a 'perfect' being, for they undergo a continuous unfolding or on-going awakening to the presence of the Soul. Although the word Wholeness is one which best describes Unividual consciousness, nothing is complete, for revealing THIS is a constant innate process.

Intuition and Synchronicity

The Unividual flows with Life in such a way that intuition and synchronicity become increasingly normal. If we are open to seeing, then we will see, and there are many ways in which we can see. For the expanding human consciousness, the world is full of pointers, signs and messages which appear to support the expansion of one's consciousness. Every second of everyday reveals THIS.

Intuition is often an immediate inner knowing. And yet it is not always instant, for sometimes it may take time to fully solidify in consciousness. To the mego, intuition was a strange, occasional hunch in the form of an inner voice or a gut feeling. In the early stages of development, it is more shocking and mysterious, and has more of a 'wow' factor. In these early appearances, intuition provides momentum for the recognition of existence beyond the mego. Intuition isn't consciously brought about through the process of individual thought, yet it clearly and powerfully impacts it, like an unexpected visitor who is found to be your closest and most trusted guide and friend.

For the Unividual, the presence of intuition is comfortable because the mind is steady, spacious and flexible, and therefore more receptive to the ebbs and flows of energy. A sudden pulse of energy-information still enters consciousness before the thought appears in the mind, but as awakening continues, intuition becomes increasingly normalised. The gap between the observer and the intuition reduces, and a calm, healthy balance ensues. It's not that intuition completely dissolves, but rather that intuition is realised to be a natural tool of awakening to the presence of the Soul.

The energy-information gained from the recognition of intuition can be a small matter or a whole host of information, as if 'downloaded' in a few seconds. By continuing to listen to intuition, we recognise its value and help as to how things may become clear, seen or known. It can then be used as a 'tool' of consciousness. It is definitive, unwavering and always helpful. So, given time and practice, intuition becomes accepted as a solid aspect of who You are.

In the lateral mind space of the mego, knowing is essentially a recalling of details and events stored in the physical brain, combined with original residual feedback from the physical senses. When the same mind-energy which brings this about is used to project not 'into' the toolbox of the brain, but into the dimension of the Soul, then intuition appears.

Intuition is the voice of the Soul. It is the tool the mego uses to find Awareness, and the mechanism which allows the Unividual to bloom in consciousness. Real intuition which comes from being open and attentive is consistently helpful and true. The beneficial outcomes it points to and provides are a reminder of the Intelligence at the core of Being.

Intuition plays an increasingly prominent role in the Unividual's awakening. It appears as and when required, the gift of 'seeing' and 'knowing' of One-duality. In the blanket anonymity of Non-duality there is no Soul and no 'other', so such gifts of the Soul are overlooked, gifts which provide a contribution to the betterment of *all* humanity. If we can use such gifts to prevent, heal, counsel or understand, then surely, they mustn't be denied, but utilised to their fullest potential.

Synchronicities are occurrences which have interconnected meaning and a non-apparent common cause. When everything is realised to be One, THIS is clear. These synchronicities occur because they are clues to the pathway of the Soul. Signs, people, places or events come into your life to help you learn and grow, to challenge or to give peace and clarity. Each day we encounter meaningful coincidences but these are seldom recognised as the wonderful opportunities they truly are. We close our minds to what IS because we have already defined these 'coincidences' as random appearances, or illogical impossibilities, because they are outside of the comfort zone of how we prefer to see reality. In doing so, we overlook their real meaning. Every synchronicity is a window to the dimension of the Soul.

Consciousness attracts consciousness. Frequency attracts frequency. Whatever you think, feel or say is an electromagnetic field of energy which emanates from you, and resonates with like-minded fields of energy. The dual law of sympathetic resonance points to THIS, how under the right conditions, one note struck on a piano transfers sound-energy to the equivalent stationary string on another nearby instrument, causing it to 'sing' the same note. That is sympathetic resonance, and it is similar to what takes place in human consciousness. When You are 'tuned' to the Heart Stream of Consciousness, You will sing its song.

Synchronicity and intuition are part of the fabric of Soulness, for they are inter-dimensional clues to the interconnectedness of humanity, and indeed of all life. When we ignore or live in a consciousness which negates their existence or denies THIS multi-faceted unity, can it be truly Whole? Clear examples in the context of this book are identification rooted in the separate mind of mego or the negation of the Unividual persona – an idea which comes from clinging to the experience of Awareness. Both are incomplete and fail to realise the multidimensional Reality of the Whole. Yet both experiences consider themselves to be already whole. It is the Whole-part Unividual which recognises Animal and Spirit, duality and Non-duality, which compounds THIS sense of Wholeness in human consciousness. It is the Unividual who remains open to the reality that it is only just becoming conscious of the Divine mystery of Life and *awakening*. It is neither dormant nor awakened, neither ignorant nor enlightened. It is the Unividual which unifies and compliments all dimensions of the human being, in the living awareness that it is a unique worldly expression of the One. The Unividual is aware that Spirit-Being-Awareness is the coreless core and it shares THIS One-duality via earthly expression. It is Awareness which gives birth to the interconnected child of the Universe. Looking back at the metamorphosis of consciousness, there was the **you** of the individual mego, then a **YOU** of Universal Awareness, and now a **You** which is the integral expression of a Unividual.

Sharing is the nature of the Soul. To share there must always be two. To recognise the One, there must be duality. To become, there must be some 'thing' wanting and something 'other' to be. To be the One as nobody, no-mind and no-thing negates the sacred multiplicity emerging from the One. If this idea of nothingness is not let go, it becomes yet another form of denial, exclusion and stagnation. To live the realisation of the One with the recognition of the many is the loving, wholesome and all-inclusive way of the Human Spirit and indeed, the entire Universe. One-duality is both the consciousness of the Soul and the wholistic identity of the Unividual, and the stepping stone for the evolution of human consciousness.

14

∞ One-duality ∞

So, by stripping back the mego to the source of the mind we find Universal Awareness. THIS has been pointed to world over by many names; Essence, Source, No-mind, Emptiness, the Void, God, the Divine, pure Consciousness, the SELF, the Absolute, Being and many more.

There are common understandings of what all these words point to. To simplify and unify them provides us with the realisation that they all point to the same coreless core, the founding and all-permeating pure Energy Consciousness of Life itself. It is impossible to absolutely define or precisely conceptualise exactly what THIS is, for although mind is in it and of it, the mind arises from it as an expression too. THIS cannot be pinned down, located and absolutely identified, for it is all, the incorruptible Whole.

In Buddhist literature, the Bodhisattva Avalokita says:

Listen Shariputra, form is emptiness, emptiness is form, form does not differ from emptiness, emptiness does not differ from form. The same is true with feelings, perceptions, mental formations, and consciousness.

The journey to the essence of the mind is like the allegory of a fruit worm burying into an apple, uncovering the layers of what it is. The apple that was initially experienced as a colourful skin with a sweet odour and a protruding wooden stalk, is next revealed to have a tasty fleshy interior, before being seen to have an ovary or protective core, and the hard husk or seed within that core. Only from experiencing all layers or dimensions of the apple does the worm get to know what the whole apple really is.

Now when the little worm exits the tunnel and crawls back out of the skin, the apple is still the apple, but is now seen by the fruit worm as a totality, with no one part of the experience being the whole on its own, and all parts contributing to the whole apple.

THIS points to the all-inclusive all-permeating presence of Being, and not to a specific exclusivity or negation of 'not this' and 'not that'. It is THIS, THIS and THIS. It is always here and now, always THIS, the One-dual reality of the Soul.

To confine consciousness to duality requires a subject and an object, a subjective identity and an objective 'other'. Awareness in the human experience is the vibrant, silent bare-minded state wherein object and subject arise together without separation. Awareness has no separation, no thought arising, no words, no concepts and no person to express it, and yet it is here before the arising of sense or thought. The individual mind of the mego is only dualistic, and cannot get THIS.

There is no becoming Awareness, for Awareness is already here and now, so there is no becoming what already *IS*. Awareness is not who You are, but what YOU, WE, and EVERY-THING *IS*. However, there is on-going Change and Action in the Universe arising from Awareness flowing and appearing in many dimensions, otherwise there would be no Life, no sharing and no expression. To the Soul it is the emergence of Awareness through Unividual consciousness which unfolds conscious evolution, and Authentic Human Being-ness.

If we look back in world history, THIS is evident. We needed to experience the pain and suffering of wars to realise they are contrary to the Heart Stream of Consciousness, and provide no answer, no long-term solution. We needed to reach the abyss of self-destruction to realise things had to change, and that in order to do so, human consciousness had to grow and evolve. We needed to look at what we had done to the planet to recognise that we were destroying our habitat, and neglecting our world. We needed to envisage Earth's plight before we could look to evolve a sustainable future. Human consciousness has clearly shifted on waves. Seeing through the dysfunctional world of the materialistic mego, humankind is presently evolving a new global consciousness. THIS is being revealed in the world through the actuality of awakening to Soulness.

Science is catching up too. Only five decades ago, the notion that space was completely empty was widely accepted, whereas today, Science tells us that THIS empty space is full of an inter-connected living intelligent pulsating essence. Not that long ago, THIS was only the claim of mystics and sages who had seen through the veil of the physical and mental dimensions.

As Max Planck, the originator of quantum theory expressed so well:

All matter originates and exists only by virtue of a force... We must assume behind this force the existence of a conscious and intelligent Mind. This Mind is the matrix of all matter.

Not long ago, the idea that there is an inner experience available to us all which has the potential to change the way we live was pretty much unheard of. Today both Science and the shared revelations from consciousness-related experiences agree that by understanding the interconnected nature of the Universe we can learn to influence the physical reality of the world. How amazing is that? These are clearly times of Action and Change.

The nature of space is pure energy Consciousness. Every object, including You, consists of unknown and unimagined possibilities, for Consciousness is not fixed or belonging, only confined by the dimensional view of the experiencer. In reality, it is the root, flow, presence and potential. We have the sacred birthright to choose how THIS appears as our earthly reality. Consciousness is Whole, while at the same time multidimensional and layered, so the options are unknown and unlimited. When driven by materialism and selfishness, consciousness appears as the mego which sells its soul to inequality and personal gain. But there is so much more to THIS.

The nature of One-duality is that You allow Life to take You to where You need to be, to do what You need to do for the Whole of Life. A Whole You are inseparable from. In being what You Authentically are, You are revealing the Universal Intelligence of Life. THIS is what takes place in the world when You are in conscious harmony with the Whole. You cannot grasp THIS. Action and Change will one day become as natural as sleeping, walking or breathing. Your expression of THIS flows through You, as You follow the Soul and share the unique song only You can sing.

In One-duality it is not who does what which matters, for Unividual Action benefits and supports the well-being of all. When you are infused by THIS, You will be inspired to Act, not to have or do for one's own sake, but to share the song of your Soul, which exemplifies the Unividual Human Being.

Your Soul Acts from the primary qualities of Being, which are Intelligent Love and Peace of Mind, and in doing so, opens the pathway to our evolutionary potential. Abundance arises from the Soul's intrinsic alignment with the Heart Stream of Consciousness, and the materialisation of THIS in the physical world. When you are out of alignment with THIS flow, then the soul is unknown and hidden, for consciousness is being dominated by the mego. As we expand and evolve, our nature is to harmonise with Life, and as we do, we awaken to the Whole of Life, the Oneness of All. When THIS is grounded in consciousness, the mego has been stripped naked, exposed, and accepted. Now the mego has been purged, transformed and integrated into the true persona's Whole view of Conscious Living.

Abundance is only ever Authentic if it comes about from, and for, the all-inclusive Whole, for then it is a true sharing of prosperity. The Soul is conscious of its Abundance, and how sharing accelerates the worldly manifestation of Love. To live THIS, it requires a continuous uninterrupted flow of consciousness through all dimensions of being, wherein the Universe You are consciously inseparable from, is also your closest friend and not an obstacle to find or to overcome.

I think the most important question facing humanity is, 'Is the Universe a friendly place?' This is the first and most basic question all people must answer for themselves. For if we decide that the Universe is an unfriendly place, then we will use our technology, our scientific discoveries and our natural resources to achieve safety and power by creating bigger walls to keep out the unfriendliness and bigger weapons to destroy all that which is unfriendly and I believe that we are getting to a place where technology is powerful enough that we may either completely isolate or destroy ourselves as well in this process.

If we decide that the Universe is neither friendly nor unfriendly and that God is essentially 'playing dice with the universe', then we are simply victims to the random toss of the dice and our lives have no real purpose or meaning. But if we decide that the Universe is a friendly place, then we will use our technology, our scientific discoveries and our natural resources to create tools and models for understanding that Universe; because power and safety will come through understanding its workings and its motives. God does not play dice with the Universe.

– Albert Einstein

The primary qualities of Being are Intelligent Love and Peace of Mind, and being conscious of THIS You recognise and actualise your part in the mysterious Divine Universal plan. You intuitively share THIS by being You. You flow with the Heart Stream of Consciousness in the knowingness that THIS is the core and all-permeating presence of Universal Intelligence.

Humanity is stepping into One-duality. THIS is not some

abstract idealistic fantasy, but the conscious meeting of Human and Being, our awakening to the presence of the Soul, and another chapter in the infinite expression of the Sole Cosmic Constant. The individual-based duality of the mego has fallen away, and as the Non-dual Universal is grounded, the One-dual Unividual establishes THIS in the world.

These are incredible and dangerous times in our history, and yet all chaos is a window of opportunity. As the crisis in human consciousness escalates, as the 'old' falls away and our interconnectedness becomes increasingly evident, the Unividual exemplifies an intelligent collective intention. Your integrity and availability to take part in THIS is what opens the doors to Action and Change. It is human consciousness, emerging from the hybrid homogenisation of individuality and Universality which manifests in the world for the Whole. In 2015, THIS is a melting of hearts and minds and a transformation of human consciousness on an unprecedented scale.

You are a Spiritual Activist, a Universal Warrior, for You are willing, open and available to the possibilities of Change and Action so that a safe world and a new humanity can emerge. It is the Unividual Soul, conscious of the Divine Reality, who, with the help and support of fellow Souls, facilitates THIS without needing to plan or specify an outcome. Trusting and allowing THIS to emerge from the depths of consciousness permits a natural unified solidarity, a synergy of Wholeness which has the potential to transcend the density of beliefs and patterns which previously held us back.

Synergy is "the interaction of elements that when combined produce a total effect that is greater than the sum of the individual elements." Like sharing, synergy is an energy of awakening, for it supports collective growth through cooperation. When You share You receive. Through sharing experiences, ideas and creativity, we can truly inspire one another, and consciously collaborate to make a lasting difference. That is why

One-duality is the cornerstone for building a symbiotic or mutually beneficial global reality.

One-duality is consciousness which does not need to identify or non-identify, and in THIS acceptance, both the seeking of somebody and the non-seeking of nobody dissolve to reveal Soulness. Then You will be getting on with THIS. You will be doing THIS. You will be sharing THIS. THIS is why You are here, and what You came here for. THIS is the emergence of *what-YOU-really-are in* the unbridled freedom and conscious expression of the Unividual You.

Drop all ideas, drop all versions, and let go of all preferences. You have a wonderful opportunity. An opportunity which is so unimaginable it cannot even be decided. It is possible to have a world based in healing, harmony and balance. If we all realise THIS, then it will come. It will come because You are here and THIS is always here.

The Spiritual regeneration of Earth requires the sharing of ideas, discoveries and resources. The mego will not truly share, but secretly hoard. The Unividual, conscious of the One-dual nature of the Universe, naturally shares. It's not that hard to imagine what the world could be like, if THIS consciousness was engaged and all resources were shared by the Whole. Starting with those in real need, we could rid the world of so many problems.

The Insanity of Humanity

Presently, it is estimated by www.Water.org that 750 million people do not have access to safe water – that's 1in 9 of the world's population. Inadequate drinking water, sanitation, and hand hygiene kills an estimated 842,000 people every year globally, or approximately 2,300 people per day through diarrhoea. Every single minute one child dies of a water-related disease.

Now, it is common to want to avoid or ignore these facts and figures, because if you have a sense of the brotherhood of humanity, they are difficult to swallow. But just imagine if it was your child, your partner, your family, your village or country that was affected in such a devastating way. How would you feel then? What steps would you take? Just how far would you go to remedy the situation? What if you could do nothing more without the compassionate help of others? The way forward is not acceptance alone, but to Act from acceptance. In this case Action requires the redistribution of time, energy and resources; a sharing to facilitate Change that is so desperately required in the world today. Does any individual need $1 billion? Does any company really need to make a profit of 10, 20, 30 or 40 billion dollars? Of course it can be seen with the present global commercial structure there could well be the need for reinvestment, expansion and speculation, but even so are such huge profits a requirement to 'success'? The simple and clear wisdom of the sharing nature of the Soul has always been here.

When someone steals another's clothes, we call them a thief. Should we not give the same name to one who could clothe the naked and does not? The bread in your cupboard belongs to the hungry; the coat unused in your closet belongs to the one who needs it; the shoes rotting in your closet belong to the one who has no shoes; the money which you hoard up belongs to the poor.
– Basil of Caesarea.

The truth of sharing is not about what is given, but what is kept by whom and why. What is the true source of the sharing? What do you really need? And beyond that need, can it be used to help the Whole?

The incredible amount of waste in the western world is a clear sign of madness. As much as half of all the food produced in the world ends up as waste. Half of all food bought in Europe and the US is thrown away. According to a 2012 report in The Guardian newspaper:

...about 550bn cubic metres of water is wasted globally in growing crops that never reach the consumer. Carnivorous diets add extra pressure as it takes 20-50 times the amount of water to produce 1 kilogramme of meat than 1kg of vegetables; the demand for water in food production could reach 10–13 trillion cubic metres a year by 2050. This is 2.5 to 3.5 times greater than the total human use of fresh water today and could lead to more dangerous water shortages around the world...

Now wait a minute, so as a race of beings, firstly we are not sharing the resource of fresh water with those whose lives it would save, but additionally by 2050 we will be wasting more than the same volume of water on the creation of a food supply half of which will end up in the garbage? Then we are clearly wasting human lives.

Then there's the animals' lives issue. I am not going to cast a view on who should eat what, as I realise it's a complex and highly emotive issue unlikely to be resolved except by human evolution. However, to take the lives of animals and then for that life to be wasted and simply thrown out with the trash? It's lunacy. The way the human world is presently working is madness. The rich are getting richer while the poor are dying almost unnoticed.

For a new birth, a metamorphosis of human consciousness, there must be a shedding, a giving way. For One-duality to be prevalent, the mego in all forms will need to fall away. Any mode of consciousness which does not bring people together is fatally flawed. Materialism and monstrous profiteering will collapse in time, because they are at odds with Divine Intelligence, unnatural and cannot be sustained. The multinational conglomerates are the hierarchy of the dying breed, and are doing all they can to hold on to their disintegrating identities.

As the Italian missionary and journalist Piero Gheddo pointed out so clearly:

Why are poor people more ready to share their goods than rich people? The answer is easy: The poor have little to lose; the rich have more to lose and they are more attached to their possessions. Poverty provides a deeper motivation for understanding your neighbours, welcoming others and attending to those who are suffering. I would go so far as to say that poverty helps you understand what happiness is, what serenity is in life.

You cannot buy your Soul, but you can deny its presence through the disunion of unconscious action.

To understand what the One-dual meaning of sharing is, we must realise that it is not primarily about what is being shared, but the intention behind the sharing. Each one of us can share, but we can only share that which we know we already have. That is we must know we have the 'something' before we can share it. The One-dual sharing of the Soul manifests in a multitude of ways. There is something to share each and every day. In One-duality sharing appears intuitively, through the open-minded availability of human consciousness. You can share your time, energy, resources in an infinite number of ways. And likewise, You will automatically receive from each and every sharing.

One-dual sharing is a natural process, as natural as it was for the mego to seek its source, and as natural as it is for Universal Intelligence to be lived in the world through the persona of the Soul. The movement into One-duality is the awakening to the presence of the Soul. Yes, we are waiting for a Soul to appear, but the Soul I refer to is not a Messiah or a Buddha, but a living Unified World Soul, a conscious unification present in the One-dual consciousness of a growing number of Human Beings. We are in effect, building a bridge between Humanity and Being, a gateway for consciousness which will allow an unprecedented freedom of transparency and exchange, and a pathway for providing benefit to the Whole. Each Soul which takes part is equivalently a stone in that bridge of Souls, a part-contributor, and a co-creator in the Divine plan.

One-duality is appearing now because of the space opening in human consciousness. In time THIS new consciousness could bring about a unified understanding between all religions, all countries, and common global political and social reform. Given more time, and more conscious contributors like You, THIS will lead to Unification and the solidification of a deep collective purpose.

15

∞ Soulness ∞

Soulness is the consciousness of the Soul. THIS allows a Human to see and be aware of all dimensions of Consciousness. The body is seen, the mind is seen, Spirit known and the Soul lives THIS. It is not a question of eradication of any 'part', but a loving transmutation arising from the grounded acceptance, merging and blending in consciousness of the Universal-Individual or Unividual. It is THIS convergence of inner and outer being which provides the momentum for conscious evolution in our world.

As the mego is a partial, ever-separate and conditioned personality, and the non-mego negates the existence and unique action of the individual, the persona of the Soul arises from the knowledge, experience and living acceptance of all dimensions. As THIS emergence takes place, the persona appears as the foreground of consciousness, and it is through THIS Authentic identity that Being flows into the world of form, delivering wholistic Action and Change.

The process of awakening means that You are awakening to the presence of the Soul. You are not 'awakened' or 'perfected', for these are mind-based conclusions or 'endings', and yet neither are You incomplete. THIS is beyond thought or logical deduction. By letting go of your non-identity as the Non-dual experience, You live it. Living on Earth in a body with a mind, while conscious that YOU are Spirit, You are continuously awakening without seeking. You are living the awakening. All form is in the process of THIS awakening to Spirit. That's why You are here. Sharing THIS in the world is the natural expression of who You are.

You are formless Being expressing in Human form. Both

Being and Human are true and experienced. The One sees the One and the many see the many. The One-dual sees the One and the many as the Whole, and each Soul realises that it is a Whole-part. To deny any inherent part is to overlook the living presence of the Whole.

The Soul is not in you, it's more true to say that you are in your Soul. After the dense form of the human body, there is a primary layer of energy extending approximately 5-10cm outside of the physical limits of the body, which is known as the first layer of the human energy field. Keeping to the context of this book, there is also a Soul energy 'body' within which the physical body is held. One day, even if it's when your awareness of the physical dimension comes to an end, the Body-Mind-Spirit relationship will become clear. The Soul will be fully known and sensed, and THIS will be evident and undeniable.

The wholistic mind of the Soul

In consciousness which is awakening to the reality of the Soul, or Soulness, the mind will begin to be sensed outside of the body as well as inside. It is not limited to the head or the heart. It is both and more. When you realise mind exists outside of the body, then effectively You are becoming increasingly engaged with Universal Intelligence. Try it. Instead of believing that the mind is confined to the limitations of the physical body, try really sensing from within and beyond the body.

To do this, breathe, relax, and be still. Let all thoughts dissipate into the nothingness. When you are ready, move your consciousness outwards. Don't force it, rather relax into it. There is no disconnection, but a relaxing expansion, a natural flow. Expand the energy of mind outside the confines of the body. You can do this because 'mind' is not limited to the confines of the physical body. The expansion of mind-energy allows us to see the real source of Mind, which in its unblemished state, is pure energy Consciousness.

When I first became conscious of my Soul during a seizure in 2007, it was abundantly clear that the body was a vehicle, and not the wholistic truth of Life itself. The mind I had 'thought' with was seen through and transcended. I realised that living in the beauty of the Soul was a reality we all have access to each and every day. It is going on in every moment whether we realise it or not. Once you know THIS from experience and knowledge, then everything starts to Change. The wonderful thing about awakening to the presence of the Soul is that it is increasingly lived by You in the world. You are Living THIS mystery.

All dimensions of the Body-Mind-Spirit triad of human existence are connected and interrelated. They each require one another for existence in our earthly human form. To be conscious of one of them without the presence of the other two is a movement away from our inherent Wholeness. To see them and to know them, without deciding or confining their unrealised potential is the way for humankind to evolve, and THIS is the consciousness of the Soul – or Soulness.

THIS is the meeting of the inner and the outer, the lower and the higher, the darkness and the light. Do you really think Intelligence only belongs to the human race? Long before we were here, long before any single cell life form existed, Universal Intelligence was present as it is here and now. Expansion and sharing were the modes of expression, and they remain so to THIS day. They always will be. Long after we're gone, when our world of form is no longer here, Universal Intelligence will still be THIS.

Soulness arises from the recognition, realisation and actualisation of Human and Being, form and formlessness, Animal and Spirit, the many and the One. It is neither one nor the other, but both and neither. THIS is not a decision, or a clinging, or a need. It is the natural expression of Universal Intelligence as lived and shared in the evolution of human consciousness.

The twenty-first century is a time of chaos and collapse, of redress and reconciliation, of discovery and growth. All of these are simultaneously necessary in order to free ourselves from the outdated beliefs, systems and structures of the mego. The 'rub' of consciousness, of the old receding as the new emerges, is underway. We need to face and end humanity's collective unconscious actions in order to embrace the possibility of a world abundant with transparency, joy and hope. Our race is becoming aware of its founding interconnectedness with the totality of Life, and THIS is the only way humankind will heal, grow and survive. What a wonderfully mysterious canvas of opportunity. You are here taking part in THIS and can contribute more than you can possibly imagine.

The consciousness of the Soul is present in every single human being to the same intensity, but to varying degrees of awareness or recognition. As we evolve, we realise that the Soul is the bridge of consciousness binding the Individual and the Universal. For when the individual conditioned personality is believed to be your entire identity, then the soul lies buried or to a great extent, unrecognised. The unrecognised soul has been forgotten or overlooked for so long, that it has become synonymous with the individual mind of mego. THIS is our error and the historical consequences for humanity and the world are all too evident.

The diving of the mego into Awareness initially leads to the Non-dual realisation that all is One. All is One, and nothing 'other' is. Another way to explain this is to say that Awareness sees Awareness and 'dissolves' into itself when there is nothing 'there' to obstruct THIS. When we are ready to let go of the experience of non-identity, that is when the Non-dual has truly grounded in the One-duality of the Human Being, then it may be lived through the wholistic expression which naturally emerges.

Without space, the stars would not appear in the night sky. And yet, although full of space themselves, they appear and act as stars. They live and die as stars. It's not a problem. Your Soul is like one of the many billions of stars in the Universe that lives in space, is made from space, and yet has an identifiable physical form and an identifiable luminosity. Human consciousness went astray when we took it upon ourselves to deny the universal Reality that *all* life is fundamentally One, equal and inseparable. Only when we believed we were separate could we see and live separation. The mego arose from a mind-based distortion of the sacred purpose and nature of duality. Duality without the presence of the Non-dual is incomplete. So too is any idea of Non-duality which is not all-inclusive of the many appearances or parts of THIS.

As the SELF *is* All, then All *is* the SELF.

The quote at the beginning of the book is a timely reminder:

Some there are that prize Non-dualism, others hold to dualism. They know not the Truth, which is above both.
– Advadhut Gita (1.34)

In Soulness, Life is known to be One without trying to 'be' One. The One is Spirit, and the Soul is Spirit, so there is no clinging to the intellectual understanding of Being or to the experience of Oneness. THIS needs no proof, no justification, and seeks no approval. You will not need to seek confirmation from another. You do not seek identity, for it is here and now, being lived by the persona of the Soul. You do not seek non-identity, for it is also here. All is THIS, and undeniably here and now.

The anonymity of Universal Awareness is only 'seen' without the presence of a wandering and doubting individual mind. Now it is clear that the 'I-less' Non-dual experience of blanket anonymity is a catalyst for the emergence of a multidimensional consciousness, a persona through which Universal expression is alive in the world.

Gautama Buddha did not deny the presence of the Soul:

...there are those who accuse me falsely of being a nihilist, of teaching the non-existence and annihilation of the Soul. That is what I am not and do not teach.
– Paul Brunton – {Inspiration and the Overself p.105}

Buddhism does not deny the existence of a persona in a relative empirical sense. It only attempts to show that it does not exist in an ultimate or absolute sense, as is the same with all 'things'. A soul-less philosophy does not explain the mode and manner of the continuance of knowledge and experience when the Dalai Lama is reborn and rediscovered. According to the Dalai Lama himself, *"Sentient beings come to this present life from their previous lives and take rebirth again after death."* And yet, in the Buddhist philosophy of the ultimate reality or Absolute, there is no rebirth. This does not explain the paradox of the Dalai Lama's statement, or the many stories of reincarnation. One way that paradoxes such as these can be resolved is through Soulness. The consciousness of the Soul sees that both of these are true. In the cycle of karma and rebirth, there is the presence of a reincarnated soul. In the Absolute, nothing is but THIS. When a soul is reborn into form, it brings with it subconscious traces of past consciousness. Any parent who has two or more children knows that although they are born into the same culture, given the same upbringing, the same education and a consistent parental love, they carry their own birth-less originality.

Identifying with Awareness is a duality. The negation or idea that the dimensions of Body and Mind are illusory creates another form of separation. This is why when individual consciousness realises its pure-minded Essence, there is no individual perception, simply immersion. Duality becomes impossible, and seemingly non-existent. Likewise Non-duality is unreal to the individual mind. Soulness sees that any perceived knowing comes from the location or non-location of consciousness. Consciousness is infinite and unlimited, and so are its possibilities.

The nature of rebirth is not dissimilar to being swallowed by a black hole, if we imagine that when this takes place, all form is broken down into its lowest common denominator, before becoming reformed with a different physical appearance in a different place and time. THIS, found in and beyond all form, pulls itself into itself, rather like a black hole, which of course is just another expression of THIS.

Words, worlds and visions

Everything is energy. Consciousness is pure Energy. The further we reveal THIS, the more words are understood, and the more their apparent differences converge. All words appear from stillness, and yet Authentic words which express the primary qualities of Being share a discernible value.

Getting to know the Soul is the on-going reality of multidimensional life. The awakening does not mean or suggest that one is enlightened, and nor does it hold onto the idea that the journey is over. Once seeking has faded, then Conscious Living is just beginning. Conscious Living reveals the impulse of Universal Intelligence through a wholistically-minded Unividual. Action leads to Change which leads to Action, the Universal flow of cause and effect. THIS is the infinite cycle of the universe, and for the Human Being in the world of form, there are natural dimensional laws which apply to our physical dimension. These same laws are at odds with the non-physical dimension. The earlier example of giving in the physical dimension leading to the appearance of less is a limited view. Giving as an expression and Action of the Soul is simultaneously compensated through Abundance in the non-physical.

As I described in Naked Being #133:

Naked Being is the most un-mathematical reality. It gives, yet in the act of giving, it simultaneously grows, defying logic. For how can you give something and at the same time increase in it? Only because you are not giving a quantifiable measurement of something, but sharing what YOU are with who You are, and [THIS] is Intelligent Love.

Anyone who shares Authentically is awakening to the infinite treasure of their Soul.

It is the Soul's role to manifest THIS. If we overlook THIS, humankind will disappear off the face of the planet. If we realise THIS, then as a race of beings, we will align human consciousness with Universal Intelligence, and with it, begin to uncover the limitless possibilities of Consciousness.

The creation myth of the 'Garden of Eden' can be seen as the history of the Soul. The 'fall from grace' through 'sin' can be seen as the descent of human consciousness from Soulness to the disconnected dualistic state of the mego. The arrival of the mego (symbolised by the serpent) leads to the loss of humanity's awareness of the Soul. In terms of the flow of life, human consciousness stepped out of the Heart Stream of Consciousness, 'bit the apple' and in doing so, became ignorant to the living presence and expression of the Soul. As human consciousness was disconnected from the Soul, the mego assumed the foreground of consciousness, and the individual mind presumed itself and the soul to be one and the same. So, this story can be used to explain how the real consciousness of the Soul became buried in the depths of our psyche.

There are many similar stories and myths. THIS Soul consciousness we are awakening to in 2015 is mentioned in the writings of the English-educated Aurobindo Ghose or Sri Aurobindo, an Indian philosopher and yogi (1872-1950). Aurobindo's central theme was the evolution of human consciousness towards the presence of Divine life on Earth through spiritual transformation.

Below are some of his thoughts on what he calls a 'gnostic being':

The gnostic individual would be in the world and of the world, but would also exceed it in his consciousness and live in his Self of transcendence above it. He would be universal but free in the universe, individual but not limited by a separative individuality. His universality would embrace even the Ignorance around him in its larger self, but, while intimately aware of it, he would not be affected by it. The gnostic being would be in unison and communion with the Consciousness-Force which is the root of everything. In the emergence of the gnostic being, there would be the hope of a more harmonious evolutionary order in terrestrial Nature.

These words bring us back to THIS we have overlooked, and THIS we are growing increasingly conscious of and returning to. Here are a few more telling words from a variety of sources which contain a similar message:

The purpose of our journey on this precious Earth is now to align our personalities with our souls. It is to create harmony, cooperation, sharing, and reverence for Life. It is to grow spiritually. This is our new evolutionary pathway.
– Gary Zukav

First we receive the light, then we impart the light, thus we repair the world.
– The Kabala

You are here to enable the divine purpose of the universe to unfold. That is how important you are!
– Eckhart Tolle

Theosophist author Alice A. Bailey described the evolution of human consciousness as: *"The bringing about of at-one-ment, and the identification of the personality with the central self, the soul."*

Or returning once more to the words found in the closing

lines of the Advadhuta Gita, a sacred text regarded by some scholars to be one of the greatest works of Advaita Vedanta or Non-duality: *"I am the Infinite in my Soul"*.

What all these quotes have in common, is they all point to the awakening Soulness presently unfolding in the world. They all come from a deep sense of sharing the Individual-Universal relationship which is brought into the world through You. It takes Non-dual Being and the dual Human to converge to manifest THIS step. When Being is Authentically expressed through You, THIS appears in the world.

So, to summarise, Soulness is the dimension of human consciousness through which the essential qualities of Being flow into the world. Each awakening Unividual naturally contributes to the world of form. As the old established worldview consciousness breaks down, the new simultaneously appears, unfolding unlimited and untouched evolving potentials.

This is how the American author and futurist Barbara Marx-Hubbard described the work which lies ahead in her book, *Emergence – The Shift from Ego to Essence*:

The work becomes a maturation process. The local self becomes the emissary and implementer of essential levels of awareness. The unification of the local self with the Essential Self for the purpose of re-patterning and expanding the external world weaves a new social wineskin. This expansion will enable us to access untapped natural resources. We will be able to afford the life which has been essentially given to us. If we live as a sacred act, we will manifest heaven on earth.

To establish THIS, it will take You and others like You. It is no one in particular and everyone together which opens the door to such bright possibilities. The future is unfolding here and now in THIS very moment. THIS moment remains the window to seeing THIS, being THIS, sharing THIS and revealing THIS in form. There is no other way. Perhaps one day the natural flow of life will no longer be obstructed by an isolated sense of self; and then THIS will be apparent.

The mego's material world of form is spiralling out of control, and yet the twenty-first century is the most remarkable time in human history. In the depths of chaos, prepare to celebrate, for when any end appears, a bright new beginning presents itself too.

To conclude YOU are THIS, I'd like to leave you with a thought provoking quote from my fictional novel, *The Soul Whisperer:*

The power of love has been replaced by the love of power. Joy has become synthetic, and is typically measured in belongings and appearances, and not in the realisation of our core being. And yet, you are Spirit – and all is not lost. For deep within you there exists an innate wisdom of what is good, true and loving. This is the consciousness of the Soul.

There will be chaos and confusion, but out of this catastrophe will come a new world (Terra Nova) and a new human – Homo Novus. You are here as witnesses and tools to that extraordinary path of evolution. All humans are potentially beautiful beings with an incredible secret, a shared secret that is so powerful it can change the way you live and the world you live in. That secret has been waiting for you to remember the truth of who you are, so that you could recognise, realise and actualise your divine inheritance; to sense in surety that you are a multidimensional being of infinite potential. That Love is your truest language. And Heart is your noblest mind.

When you look back and realise everything that passed before was a blessing, and all that is to come is necessary for your learning and growth, then truly, you will have entered the consciousness of the Soul. That time is upon us now. Today we are witnessing a new dawn for humanity, a time of hope and change. Let go of fear, for it has no place here. Breathe and outwardly embrace the sacred sense of life within. For there you will find the peace and love that all seek.

Be free. It is your birthright, your nature and your responsibility. When you are free, you cannot but help others to be free. That's how wonderfully kind and loving you are.

So the secret is out. Souls are awakening to this world. And this world is awakening to Soul. It is time to speak and act from Love and Truth, for then new life will come to one and all, and a new Earth will appear.

You are THIS!∞

16

∞ Paradoxes of the Soul ∞

The following contemplations reveal the paradoxical nature of Soulness. To get the most from them, please read each one slowly and carefully and let them 'sit' with you for a while before beginning any mental commentary.

∞

The Soul is a conscious Whole and part simultaneously, without separation.

∞

The Soul is not personal, and yet it is Yours.

∞

No Soul is identical – yet all Souls are unified.

∞

The uniqueness of each Soul is realised through the Soul-less anonymity of Awareness.

∞

Only through Oneness can the unique persona of the Soul be expressed.

∞

No Soul is the Self without awareness of its originality.

∞

The Soul is a part inseparable Whole or Whole-part.

∞

Soul Action is not the same as the action of the mego, yet they may appear the same.

∞

The Awareness of no one leads to Change in someone and others.

∞

From the desire to seek, comes desire-less-ness. From desire-less-ness comes Universal Action and Change.

∞

You cannot remember to search for the Soul. You find it, and then you remember.

∞

The more we shine, the more luminous the Soul becomes.

∞

Letting go allows you to grow.

∞

All opposites are complimentary partial truths and
simultaneously true.

∞

The idea of other becomes no other, before it is realised as both
and neither.

∞

You see what you identify with; the part, the Whole, or the
Whole-part.

∞

While it is true the Soul is within you, it is also true that you
are within your Soul.

∞

The mego acts from the head-brain, whereas the Soul Acts from
the Heart Stream of Consciousness.

∞

The mego requires no faith, and the Soul requires no belief.

∞

Awareness purges personality so that the Soul may live it
Authentically.

∞

Souls are unique patterns of a singular Consciousness.

∞

An awakening Soul is the puzzle and the piece.

∞

Fear arises in consciousness when Love is forgotten.

∞

What you believe as being true is only what is apparent to *you*. Truth is Universal.

∞

There are no longer options, simply possibilities.

∞

I alone cannot decide; I simply flow with the unfolding.

∞

My physical heart 'belongs' to this body. The Universal Heart belongs to no one, and yet lives within everyone.

∞

A conscious Soul knows that it is a Human, and *our* Being.

∞

The mego forgets what it is looking for, yet the Soul never complains.

∞

In Non-duality there is no you, but who is the one who lives this?

∞

If no one is awakened to nothing, what is conscious of the fact that 'they' themselves are awake and the perception that 'others' are not?

∞

Consciousness appears random, and yet it is the Sole Cosmic Constant.

∞

YOU were born into you, in order to find YOU, and live as You.

∞

Time only exists in a time-based reality.

∞

To hold on to anything stops you from being You.

∞

The Soul is not hungry, yet it consumes you.

∞

The evolution of human consciousness begins by looking outward, then looking inward, until you arrive at a balance where the Soul lives the inner through the outer as One.

∞

In Soulness, the persona is lived, but without a follower.

∞

Awakening to Soul is the conscious living of your incarnation.

∞

In letting go of any destination, your route opens wide up.

∞

If we stop defining, something definitive takes place.

∞

You cannot do things better without the mind, but with the clear, calm presence of Mind you can do everything better.

∞

The consciousness of the Soul lives duality knowing it to be the One.

∞

Non-duality is Awareness experiencing itself, which is a duality.

∞

Consciousness detached from the world of form is incomplete.

∞

Fulfilment follows Surrender.

∞

The Soul is 'something' conscious of everything and nothing.

∞

Each Soul is an instrument for Change and Action.

∞

Appendix i. Exercises*

There is no requirement to do these exercises, but they will be helpful to some, so I have included them in this part of the book.

Breathing exercises such as these bring about a sense of calm and spaciousness conducive to contemplation and enquiry. Mind and breath are inseparable. When you control your breath, you control your mind.

In Hindu, the art of breath control is known as *Pranayama*. The word comes from the convergence of two Sanskrit words: *Prana* which means breath or vital energy and *Ayama* which means control. So Pranayama equivalently means 'control of breath'.

In the ancient Hindu text *The Yoga Sūtras of Patañjali*, the yogic discipline of Pranayama is described as an important practice for realising expanded states of awareness, and the holding of breath as a fundamental practice for reaching Samadhi (as mentioned in Chapter 9).

In this type of conscious breathing, an inhalation fills the lungs with fresh air, and the pace, depth and retention of the incoming breath supports an efficient increase in the absorption of oxygen into the blood. Finally, the exhalation causes the expulsion of physical and mental 'toxins'. The mind naturally becomes stilled in the process. With daily practice, the body and mind becomes balanced and healthy, and consciousness becomes open, clear and transparent. Try it and see.

According to the Indian Sage Ramana Maharshi:

...breathing will naturally (and as a matter of course) lead to cessation of thought and bring the mind under control.

The mind abstracted from other activities is engaged in watching the breath. That controls the breath; and in its turn the mind is controlled.

The source can be reached by regulating the breath... Regulation

of the breath is accomplished by watching its movements.
The breath will take you all the way to Nirvana.

Even though it is right under your nose, the breath is often overlooked. I have found that it provides great benefits to the well-being of body and mind and would recommend these types of exercises. There are many, many more out there, and these exercises below are not complex. As with any 'practice' I would suggest it is helpful and beneficial at a certain point in one's journey, and not a permanent requirement.

Exercise A: Emptying the mind of blockages

1. Find a comfortable place outside, or close to fresh air, where you can comfortably sit or stand.
2. With your feet apart, stretch your arms out horizontally like a child pretending to be an aeroplane.
3. Breathe in through the nose to the slow count of 5, and visualise bright, white golden light entering the body. (As with all these exercises, be sure to breathe deeply and expand your lower belly diaphragm – not only your chest.)
4. Exhale via the mouth to the count of 10 as you visualise any clouds or residual negative energy leaving your body.
5. Don't overdo it. A dozen times maximum. If you feel dizzy or need to stop, then do so immediately. Eventually the flow coming out will become the same colour as the inflow.

Exercise B: Improving energy flow

1. Stand in a comfortable position, preferably outside or in a flow of fresh air.

2.   Bring your hands palms together in the prayer position, being careful not to interlink the fingers.

3.   While retaining the prayer position, and on the in breath, move the hands upwards until they are at full stretch above your head. Hold your arms in position as you hold your breath to the count of three.

4.   Turn your palms away from each other, while keeping your arms extended; bring them slowly down to your sides to the count of nine, as if you are swimming in the air.

5.   Bring them back to the prayer position and repeat the exercise.

6.   Again, don't overdo it, a dozen times maximum.

Exercise C: Vocal Toning – for balance and well-being

1.   Lie down on the floor, couch or bed.

2.   Relax and breathe in to the count of eight.

3.   Hold your breath to the count of 12.

4.   Now exhale, and as you do open your mouth and allow the throat to express the outgoing breath with a gentle 'AHHHH'. Let this go on as long as you feel comfortable. A good way to do this is to imagine you are trying to gargle from the base of your throat.

5.   With practice stage 4 will develop and the growling note coming from the lower part of the larynx will become louder and clearer.

6.   Again, do this no more than 5 times before stopping.

Exercise D: Visualisation of inner and outer being

1.   Find a candle and a lighter.

2.   In a quiet room, draw the curtains or turn off the lights, or both.

3. Light the candle and sit watching the candle flicker and move. Do this for ten minutes, and each time your mind wanders, think 'CANDLE' and come back to the candle.

4. When you are able to maintain focus on the candle without mental interruption for at least one minute, shut your eyes and visualise this moving image in your mind's eye as if you are dreaming the candle. When the image fades or alters, simply open your eyes and look at the physical candle which is still alight in the room. Then return to closing your eyes and seeing the flickering glowing candle in your mind's eye.

5. When you can maintain your focus on the image of the candle in your mind's eye for more than one minute without interruption, and when you feel sufficiently confident that this is the case, blow out the candle in the room.

6. Return to the candle in your mind's eye. Start to notice the qualities of the candle. The light, the multiple blending of colours, the movement of the flame. Each time your mind wanders, come back to the image of the candle with the simple thought 'CANDLE'.

7. If you practise this on a daily basis, you will be able to shut your eyes at any time and visualise the candle.

8. Eventually you will be able to see the candle in your mind's eye with your eyes wide open, and while going about life in the physical world.

*N.B – As with any breathing exercises, please use common sense and do not force yourself. Stop the exercise immediately if you feel any pain or discomfort.

Appendix ii. Web-based resources

www.AuthorJMHarrison.com – the author's official website and access to other books, blog and music.

www.sriaurobindoashram.org – free downloads of 28 volumes of Sri Aurobindo's writings.

www.ramana-maharshi.info – free Ramana Maharshi book downloads.

www.o-books.com – the foremost MBS publisher in the UK.

www.kheper.net – Alan Kazlev's thorough and informative website.

www.sacred-texts.com – the largest freely available archive of religious and esoteric literature on the Internet.

Bibliography

Books referenced in this text include:

Paul Brunton. *Inspiration and the Overself – Vol.14: Notebooks of Paul Brunton* (Larson Publications, 1988)

Paul Brunton. *Enlightenment Mind, Divine Mind – Vol.16: Notebooks of Paul Brunton* (Larson Publications, 1988)

Ramana Maharshi. *Be As You Are: The Teachings of Sri Raman Maharshi,* edited by David Godman (Arkana, 1985)

Eckhart Tolle. *A New Earth: Awakening to your life's purpose* (Penguin, 2005)

Marvin.W.Meyer (Trans). *The Secret Teachings of Jesus: Four Gnostic Gospels* (Random House, 1984)

Sri Aurobindo. *The Mind of Light* (Lotus Press 2003)

Barbara Marx Hubbard. *Emergence – The Shift from Ego to Essence* (Hampton Roads 2001)

By the same author

We Are All One – A Call to Spiritual Uprising
(2007) *paperback* (2015) *e-book (ALOL Publishing)*

Naked Being – Undressing your Mind, Transforming your Life
(2010) *paperback* (2015) *e-book (O-Books)*

The Soul Whisperer – A Tale of Hidden Truths & Unspoken
    Possibilities
(2016) *paperback and e-book (Roundfire Books)*

For further information and updates, visit the author's website at:
www.AuthorJMHarrison.com

MANTRA
BOOKS

We publish books on Eastern religions and philosophies.
Books that aim to inform and explore the various
traditions, that began rooted in East and
have migrated West.